Washington, DC
History for Kids

The Making of a Capital City

★ ★ ★   with *21* Activities

Richard Panchyk

CHICAGO REVIEW PRESS

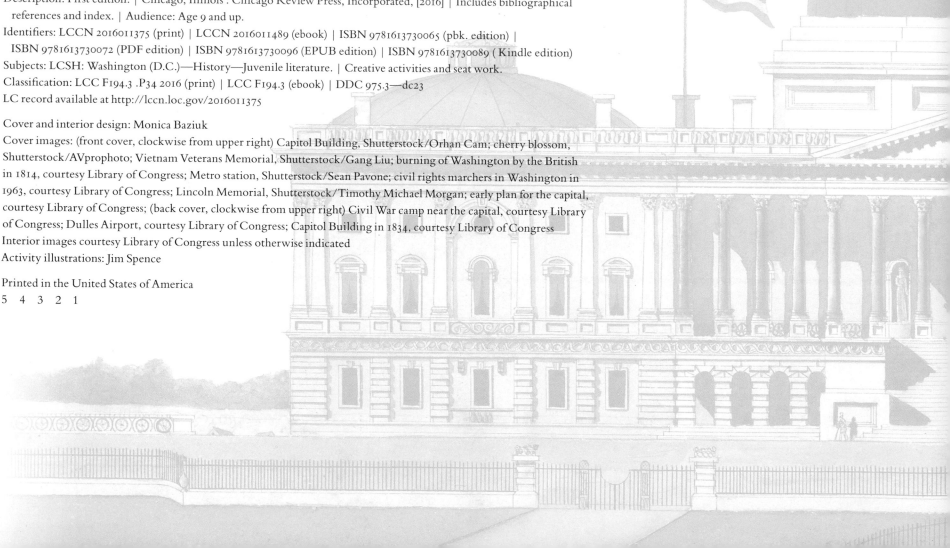

Published by Chicago Review Press, Incorporated
814 North Franklin Street
Chicago, Illinois 60610
ISBN 978-1-61373-006-5

Library of Congress Cataloging-in-Publication Data
Names: Panchyk, Richard, author.
Title: Washington, DC, history for kids : the making of a capital city with 21 activities / Richard Panchyk.
Description: First edition. | Chicago, Illinois : Chicago Review Press, Incorporated, [2016] | Includes bibliographical
    references and index. | Audience: Age 9 and up.
Identifiers: LCCN 2016011375 (print) | LCCN 2016011489 (ebook) | ISBN 9781613730065 (pbk. edition) |
    ISBN 9781613730072 (PDF edition) | ISBN 9781613730096 (EPUB edition) | ISBN 9781613730089 (Kindle edition)
Subjects: LCSH: Washington (D.C.)—History—Juvenile literature. | Creative activities and seat work.
Classification: LCC F194.3 .P34 2016 (print) | LCC F194.3 (ebook) | DDC 975.3—dc23
LC record available at http://lccn.loc.gov/2016011375

Cover and interior design: Monica Baziuk
Cover images: (front cover, clockwise from upper right) Capitol Building, Shutterstock/Orhan Cam; cherry blossom,
Shutterstock/AVprophoto; Vietnam Veterans Memorial, Shutterstock/Gang Liu; burning of Washington by the British
in 1814, courtesy Library of Congress; Metro station, Shutterstock/Sean Pavone; civil rights marchers in Washington in
1963, courtesy Library of Congress; Lincoln Memorial, Shutterstock/Timothy Michael Morgan; early plan for the capital,
courtesy Library of Congress; (back cover, clockwise from upper right) Civil War camp near the capital, courtesy Library
of Congress; Dulles Airport, courtesy Library of Congress; Capitol Building in 1834, courtesy Library of Congress
Interior images courtesy Library of Congress unless otherwise indicated
Activity illustrations: Jim Spence

Printed in the United States of America
5 4 3 2 1

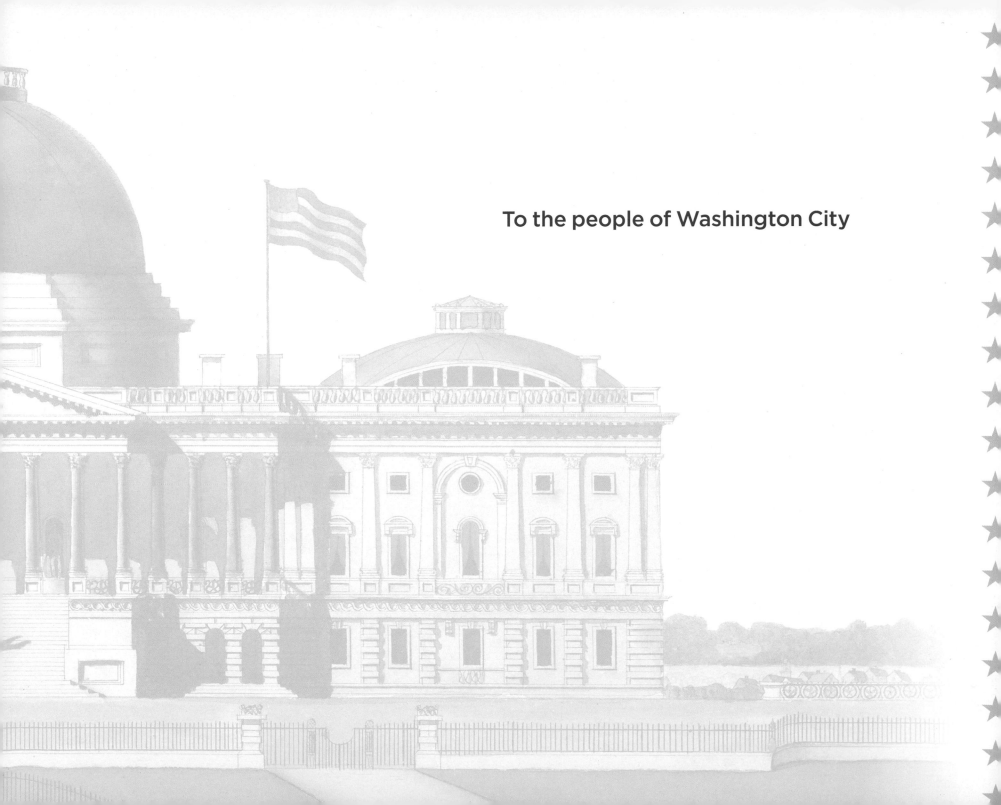

To the people of Washington City

★ Contents ★

TIME LINE VI

INTRODUCTION IX

1. A Capital Is Born, 1600–1792 1
Archaeology in Your Backyard 4
City Layout Game 9
Survey the District Diamond 12

2. Early Days, 1792–1805 15
Propose a Resolution 24

3. Washington Burns, 1805–1840 27
Create a Watermark 37
Supreme Court Scrapbook 40

4. Three Landmarks, 1840–1860 45
Then and Now Game 50
Create a Smithsonian Collection 55
Make a Cornerstone Box 60

5. Civil War Days, 1860–1880   *63*

Write a Civil War Letter   71

Design a Memorial   77

6. The Making of a Capital City,
1880–1930   *83*

Plant a Cherry Tree   86

Mall Walking Tour   91

Design a New Flag for DC   92

Draw a Political Cartoon   94

Create a Walking Tour of Your Neighborhood   97

7. Modern Washington, 1930–Present   *99*

Search for Your Family in the National Archives
   Records   111

Write Your Own Dream Speech   114

Make a Cut-and-Cover Metro Tunnel   119

Request a Name Rubbing   122

Be an Engineer   123

ACKNOWLEDGMENTS   125

RESOURCES   126

INDEX   127

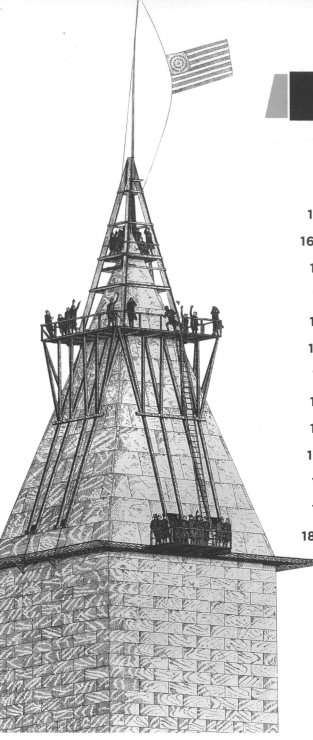

★ Time Line ★

1608 ★ Captain John Smith is the first European to explore the Washington area

1660s ★ First European settlers arrive

1748 ★ Bellhaven is founded; soon to become Alexandria

1751 ★ Georgetown is founded

1789 ★ George Washington becomes the first president of the United States

1790 ★ The Potomac is selected as the site for the future capital of the United States

1791 ★ Pierre L'Enfant begins to lay out the new city

1792 ★ Cornerstone of the White House is laid

1793 ★ Cornerstone of the Capitol is laid

1800 ★ US government officially moves to Washington

1814 ★ British burn Washington during the War of 1812

1816 ★ St. John's Church is built

1820s ★ Rebuilt and expanded Capitol is completed

1844 ★ Cannon explodes aboard the warship *Princeton*

1846 ★ District of Columbia loses part of its area, is no longer diamond shaped

1848 ★ Construction of the Washington Monument begins

1855 ★ Smithsonian "Castle" is completed

1861 ★ Civil War starts and troops begin to amass in Washington

1863 ★ New Capitol dome is completed

1865 ★ Civil War ends

　　 ★ President Lincoln is assassinated

1872 ★ "Parking Commission" is created to beautify Washington

1888 ★ Washington Monument is opened to the public

1912 ★ 3,020 cherry trees arrive as a gift from Japan

1922 ★ Lincoln Memorial is completed

1943 ★ Jefferson Memorial is dedicated

1957 ★ First segment of the Beltway opens

1962 ★ Dulles Airport opens

1963 ★ 250,000 people participate in the March on Washington, protesting for civil rights

1976 ★ Metro subway service begins

2001 ★ Terrorists crash plane into the Pentagon

2011 ★ Earthquake damages the Washington Monument

★ Introduction ★

The story of Washington, DC, is the tale of a grand vision. It shows how a swath of swampy wilderness along the Potomac River became a beautiful and majestic capital city. It's a fascinating tale that unfolded very gradually over the last three centuries. The city that was once ridiculed as an inconvenient, underpopulated, muddy mess of a place took many years to become the national capital that its designer originally envisioned. As each puzzle piece fell into place, Washington continued to evolve and grow. Along the way, many of the key moments in our country's history—both tragic and triumphant—happened here.

Today Washington, DC, is a thriving and inspiring metropolis filled with history, culture, and natural beauty. This is the story of how it got that way.

POWHATAN
this state & fashion when Capt. Smith
was deliuered to him prisoner
1607

MANNAHOACKS

P O W H A T A N

Massacack
Mewhemch
Stegara
Tanxsnitania
Shackaconia
Hasinunga
Mahaskahod
Sparkes Vhalley

The Fales
Powhatan
Cattachiptics
Passawnkack
Utenstank
Accoqueck
Fetherstone Baye
Secobeck
Martoughquaunk
Massawoteck
Anuskenoans
Booktere buff h
Sackobeck
Quirough
Burtons Mount

Arrohatteck
Crapaks
Apecant
Nechanicok
Quackcohowaon
Muttamussinsack
Chepopissou
Assurugha
Cuttatawomen

Appamatuck
Weunock
Lightbanugh
Attamuck
Poteuek
Accosttuvinck
Kupkipcock
Nandtangtacund
Ancuayeugh
Payscent
Kershacah
Mattacunt
Patawomeck
Pamacocack

Manatohunt
Mayses
Leemap
Werawahon
Matalur
Menad
Vittasunt
Vitamussack
Pissaseck
Ozeanawomen
Massalel
Matomaghao
Pamacoack
Taucenent
Namassingaks

Chawopo
Baligh
Vitamussa
Matchutt
Nawacaten
Mongoraca
Wecuppon
Nushemouk
Cinguoteck
Namassingaunt

Quiyonghcohanock
Menaskunt
Cinguoteck
Mamanassy
Poyankatank flu.
Marchpeh
Petpacs
Assareck

Nantapoyac
Mattapament
Pasaughtacock
Poruptanck
Cecomocomoco
Moyeans
Tessamatuck
Bland's C.

James towne
Mattacock
Opistoun panck
Wecuma
Nawnautacund
Aequintanacsuck
Wighcocomoco
Wosemens
Nacacchtanck
Mattapament
Downes dale

Warraskoyack
Mathomauk
Werowocomoco
Cantaunkack
Cutta tawomen
Wohco
Cowaic
Wasetup
Powhatanne
Quactatuxint

Mokete
Kishiack
Capahowasick
Nepawtacund
Ashancet
Bemako
Cinquack
Rickards clifses
Cinament
Tauerne
Winstons Iles
Brookes First
Ozinics

Nandsamund
Mattanock
Ceader Ile
Indals poynt
iffins poynt
Poynt Wefile
Poweis Iles
Barnes poynt
Poynt Pesnage

Teracosick
Shafes
Mantoughquenfd
Kecoughtan
Rickards clifses
Willoubyes flu
Attaock
Quadroque

Chesapeck
Powhatan flu.
poynt comfort
Russes Iles
Ranaishuck flu
Nause
Nantasquack
Kuskarawaock

Mertons baye
Cape Henry
Accohanack
Keales Iles
Kustarawack
Guntens Harbour

Cape Charle
Cape harbor
Reades poynt
Wohco
Tackough flu
Susquesahanough flu
Smiths fales
Susquesahanough

Smyths Iles
Washebonne C.
Wighcocomoco
Peregrins mount

MANN AHOACKS
POWHATAN

MAN GOAGS
CHILONS

SASQUESAHANOUGHS

The are a Gyant
Vchowig thus

SA - PEACK BAY

HL:

KVSKARA WA OKS

TOCK WOGHS

THE

Scale of Leagues
and halfe
Leagues

Chickahokin
Macock

Demerites tree

A Capital Is Born

1600–1792

If you had walked around in what is today Washington, DC, just 250 years ago, you would never have guessed that the nation's capital would wind up there, in the swampy emptiness along the north side of the Potomac River.

Early Residents

BY THE 1600s, Native Americans had been living in the area of the Chesapeake Bay and the Potomac River for almost 2,000 years. Closest to present day Washington was a small Algonquin village called Nacochtank. Tauxenant was a larger village near what is today Mount Vernon in Alexandria, Virginia. Other settlements included Nameroughquena, directly across the Potomac from DC in Virginia; Assaomeck, at the site of present-day Alexandria; Namassingakent, a little bit south of Alexandria; and Moyaone, across the Potomac from Tauxenant, in Maryland.

Legend has it that Native Americans used the marshy valley below Capitol Hill as a fishing ground in springtime. Tribal councils were held at the principal settlement where the Algonquin chief lived—on the peninsula where the Potomac and Anacostia Rivers meet.

As with most places along the East Coast, there was a continued influx of European settlers in the area. By the mid-18th century, the vast majority of the Native Americans in the area had been forced to retreat to the west.

The First European Settlements

THE FIRST European to explore the Washington, DC, area was Captain John Smith, who arrived in June 1608 with 14 companions. His party was the first to sail up the "Patawomeke" or Potomac River, going as far as Little Falls, about five miles north of present-day Washington. He said that there was an "abundance of fish lying so thicke with their heads above the water, as for want of nets (our barge driving amongst them) we attempted to catch them with a frying pan; but we found it a bad instrument to catch fish with." The crew fired bullets upon the water's surface, and the sound of the shots, along with their echoes, startled the Native Americans who were watching from the banks.

An English trader named Henry Fleet, who explored the same area in the 1630s while looking for furs, said, "The place is, without all question, the most healthful and pleasant place in all this country, and most convenient for habitation; the air temperate in Summer and not violent in Winter. It aboundeth with all manner of fish. The Indians in one night commonly will catch thirty sturgeons in a place where the river is not over twelve fathoms broad. And, for deer, buffaloes, bears, turkeys, the woods do swarm with them, and the soil is exceedingly fertile."

In the 1660s some Irish and Scottish settlers came to an area that is now part of DC and made a home there. In 1663, Captain Robert Troop owned property in what is now southeastern Washington. By that time, the land known today as Capitol Hill was owned by Francis Pope and

★ **Map of Virginia in 1606.**

3

Archaeology in Your Backyard

ARCHAEOLOGISTS have discovered much about DC's past through excavations at key sites. Try your hand at excavation and see what you can learn.

Artifacts from Native American cultures and early European settlements have been turning up in Washington for many years. Everything from bottles to pottery to tools has turned up in digs around the city. Archaeologists are often called in to check the ground for artifacts when a new building's foundation is being dug, and they have to work quickly to rescue what they find so that building construction remains on schedule.

You'll Need

★ Tape measure
★ 4 long nails (at least 3 inches) or 12-inch wooden dowels
★ String
★ Trowel
★ Bucket
★ Paintbrushes, various sizes
★ Notebook
★ Camera
★ Small ziplock bags
★ Permanent marker
★ Flat-bottomed sieve

Find a spot in your backyard or schoolyard (with permission) where you can dig. Measure out a 2-foot-by-2-foot square. Mark the corners with nails or dowels hammered almost all the way into the ground, and tie string from one corner to the next to set off the excavation area.

Scrape away at the surface of the ground using the trowel. Remove the loose dirt and place it into a bucket. If you spot an artifact (a piece of glass, bottle cap, coin, etc.), use a brush to clear away dirt from around the object. Note the depth at which you found it and photograph it *in situ*—where it lies. Then carefully remove it and bag it, labeling the bag with the location and date.

As you continue to scrape away, you will notice the soil changing color. This is called *stratigraphy*, or layering of the soil. Note the depth at which the change occurs and the color of each layer in your notebook. When you reach a new layer, empty the bucket into the sieve and sift to find any small artifact fragments.

Dig until you have gone down about 1 foot. By now you are probably at a level representing the surface hundreds of years ago. When you are done, refill the hole.

called "Rome." Another man, William Lang, owned land in what is now the western part of the city. It was by no means a highly populated area.

In 1748, a town called Bellhaven was founded on the Potomac in Virginia, about five miles south of what would become the city of Washington. A few years later, the name of the settlement was changed to Alexandria. It soon became a thriving and important port city, and warehouses filled with tobacco, corn, and flour lined the waterfront. George Washington, who lived in Virginia, worshipped for many years at Christ Episcopal Church, which was dedicated in 1765. In 1791, Alexandria officially became part of the District of Columbia.

Georgetown

DURING THE 18th century, the nearest settlement to the site of the nation's future capital was Georgetown, so named in honor of Britain's King George II. It was founded in 1751, when the colony of Maryland authorized five commissioners to build a town on the Potomac River, above the mouth of Rock Creek, in Frederick County.

Georgetown was to be laid out in 80 lots over 60 acres of land. The commissioners were told to purchase those 60 acres from the original landowners. Two of those owners, George Gordon and George Beall, refused to sell their land to the commissioners until it was appraised. The appraisal said the land was worth 280 pounds, so they were awarded that amount. A *survey*—a precise measurement of the land's natural features and man-made boundaries—was completed in early 1752, and Gordon and Beall were allowed to pick two lots each for their own use. Mr. Gordon agreed, but Beall was stubborn and refused. He was told he had 10 days to change his mind or he'd lose his chance. After a week, he wrote back, "If I must part with my property by force, I had better save a little than be totally demolished."

The population of Georgetown in 1800 was 2,993, and it grew quickly over the next 20 years. By 1820 the population was 7,360, and after that it leveled off, staying around 8,000 for the next 40 years.

★ The Old Stone House ★

The oldest building in Washington, DC, is located in Georgetown, and is known as the Old Stone House. Built in 1765 by a couple named Christopher and Rachael Layman, the house was made from local blue fieldstone and oak boards. The stone walls were two to three feet thick, and the floors were dirt.

Christopher died shortly after the house was built, and his widow sold it. Ownership passed from one family to another over the years as the old building continued to withstand the test of time. The Old Stone House was privately owned until 1953, when the federal government purchased the property (which was then the site of a used car dealership) for $90,000. The National Park Service opened the house to the public in 1960. It was rumored to have been George Washington's engineering headquarters, but this has never been proven.

The Old Stone House in a 1930s photograph.

Selecting a Site for the Nation's Capital

DURING THE Revolutionary War, the Continental Congress met in several different locations, for reasons that included safety. After the war ended, there was much discussion within the young republic as to where the federal government should be permanently located. New York was the largest city, but it was not centrally located. Boston was also large, but it was too far north. Among the many cities that were considered during early discussions in Congress were Kingston, New York; Annapolis, Maryland; Baltimore, Maryland; Newport, Rhode Island; Trenton, New Jersey; Williamsburg, Virginia; Wilmington, Delaware; and Philadelphia, Pennsylvania.

Debate and discussion continued for several years. Once the Constitution was adopted in 1788, Congress took up the question with a new sense of urgency, and additional locations such as Germantown and Wright's Ferry in Pennsylvania and Havre de Grace in Maryland were offered as potential sites. All in all, 24 different locations were proposed for the capital between 1783 and 1789! There was even a suggestion to have two capitals, one in the north and one in the south, so Congress could alternate between them. Philadelphia and New York badly wanted the honor, and offered to donate their existing buildings for use by the federal government.

One critic who felt the capital should be in an existing large city wrote in 1789, "When we reflect on the present state of population in the United States, nothing can be more preposterous and absurd than the idea of fixing the seat of Congress in a village, or the raising a new city in a wilderness for their residence."

In September 1789 Congress passed a bill to locate the government at Germantown, Pennsylvania, but this bill was abandoned before it became a law.

A committee had been appointed to examine the region along the Potomac, and in June 1790 Congress took up discussion of the committee's report. It recommended that the capital be located "on the eastern or northeastern bank of the Potomac," which would place the new capital only about 15 miles north of Mount Vernon, President George Washington's Virginia home.

Finally, after a month of unsuccessful, last-minute pushes for Philadelphia, Wilmington, and Baltimore, on July 9, 1790, an act "for establishing the temporary and permanent seat of government" on the Potomac passed the Senate by the narrow margin of 32–29. The bill was approved by President Washington on July 16, thus ending the seven-year-long struggle.

The Residence Act said that "a district of territory, not exceeding ten miles square, to be located, as hereafter directed, on the River Potomac, at some place between the mouths of the Eastern Branch and Connogochegue, be, and the same is hereby, accepted for the permanent seat of government of the United States." It also gave the president power to appoint commissioners who would "under the direction of the President survey, and by proper metes and bounds define and limit a district of territory, under the limitations above mentioned." The commissioners had the power to purchase land as necessary and to oversee the construction of the new city. The bill decreed that the federal government would relocate to the new capital the first Monday in December 1800, remaining in Philadelphia until that time. President Washington appointed David Stuart, Daniel Carroll, and Thomas Johnson as commissioners.

L'Enfant and the Plan for the City

BORN IN France, Pierre Charles L'Enfant had come to America in 1777 and had served as an engineer with the Patriots in the Revolution. He rose through the ranks and was well respected, and known by General Washington. After the war, Major L'Enfant designed Federal

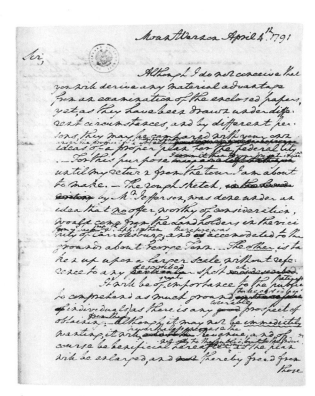

★ **A letter from George Washington to Pierre L'Enfant, April 1791.**

Hall in New York City, the first capital of the new country. He was working on a design for a mansion in Philadelphia when he was approached by George Washington to lay out the new capital city.

L'Enfant arrived in Georgetown on March 12, 1791, and immediately set about his work, assisted by a talented surveyor from Pennsylvania named Andrew Ellicott. When George Washington arrived in Georgetown on March 28, L'Enfant met him in person and gave him a preliminary report. In his report, L'Enfant described where he thought the Congress building should be located, and gave the president some of his first impressions of what the new city should look like. He explained that the city's plan should not be an ordinary rectangular grid, as that would become "tiresome." No matter how appealing it might at first look on paper, he felt it would be neither grand nor beautiful.

L'Enfant asked statesman Thomas Jefferson to send him sample city layouts from elsewhere in the world. Jefferson provided plans of European cities such as Frankfurt, Karlsruhe, Amsterdam, Strasburg, Paris, Orleans, Bordeaux, Lyons, Montpelier, Marseilles, Turin, and Milan, that he happened to have in his collection.

On June 22 L'Enfant gave a second report to President Washington, with more details and a preliminary map. He explained why some of his avenues were at different angles, telling Washington that it wasn't merely to "contrast with the general regularity" but also to provide better views of the city and to directly connect its key places. At the intersection of the avenues would be open spaces set aside for squares or parks. After receiving the president's comments, L'Enfant issued his third report, with a completed map and detailed description of its contents, on August 19. He said "the grand avenue connecting both the palace [the home of the president] and the Federal House [the meeting place of Congress] will be most magnificent and most convenient."

Earlier in the year, President Washington had referred to the new nation's capital as the "Federal City." But on September 9 the commissioners wrote L'Enfant and told him the city would be named Washington, in honor of the nation's first president. "We have agreed that the Federal District shall be called 'The Territory of Columbia,' and the Federal City the 'City of Washington,'" the commissioners wrote. The name Columbia was a reference to Christopher Columbus. "The title of the map will therefore be, 'A Map of the City of Washington in the Territory of Columbia.'" Completion of the map allowed the first public sale of lots to be held in October 1791.

The plan submitted in December by President Washington to Congress called for a great national church, five fountains, and a grand canal running through the center of the city. The L'Enfant plan featured very

★ **Andrew Ellicott.**

wide roadways: 160-foot-wide avenues, with streets between 90 and 130 feet wide.

But trouble soon arose between L'Enfant and the commissioners. It started when one of the commissioners, Daniel Carroll, had an elegant home built within the new capital for his nephew, also named Daniel Carroll. It so happened that seven feet of the building crossed over the path of what was to become New Jersey Avenue. What did L'Enfant do? He had the offending walls demolished, writing to George Washington on November 21 that "the roof now has already down with part of the brick work & the whole will I Expect be levelled to the ground before the [week] is over."

This demolition outraged both Daniel Carrolls. They felt L'Enfant had acted without consulting the commissioners. L'Enfant believed that he reported to the president, not the commissioners, and that he had the authority to act as he wished. That was the beginning of the end for L'Enfant, who had now made enemies of the commissioners. George Washington found himself in the middle of the controversy.

By January, President Washington was still of the opinion that the problem could be solved if only L'Enfant would work with the commissioners instead of trying to work around them. He did admit, though, that he didn't think this was likely to happen.

He was right. L'Enfant would have to go. In February 1792, the president wrote to L'Enfant, saying that "the continuance of your services (as I have often assured you) would have been pleasing to me, could they have been retained on terms compatible with the law." He went on to say that the only way to keep L'Enfant would be to change the commissioners, and it would not be right to do that. He closed his letter by offering "sincere wishes for your happiness

★ **The L'Enfant Plan for the nation's capital, as engraved by Andrew Ellicott.**

and prosperity." That was the end of it. L'Enfant had been fired, and his assistant Andrew Ellicott took over.

Washington was afraid that those who opposed the idea of this brand-new capital city would seize upon L'Enfant's removal and call the whole thing a failure. But that did not happen, and L'Enfant actually remained in the vicinity for the rest of his life.

The president recommended that L'Enfant be paid $2,500 or $3,000 for his services. He was offered a fraction of that, along with property in the city. He rejected both. Eight years later he finally submitted a request to Congress for $95,000. He wound up being paid $666.66 in 1810, and died penniless in 1825.

Though Washington wanted L'Enfant to have his map printed, he withheld it. Andrew Ellicott therefore made changes and improvements to the version he possessed and had the map printed in Boston in 1792, and Ellicott's version became the one upon which the development of the city was based.

Georgetown University

THE IDEA for a Catholic university in Maryland was first proposed around 1640 by Father Ferdinand Poulton, who had arrived from England in 1638. He wrote to his superiors in England with this idea and got this reply: "The hope of establishing the college which you hold forth,

City Layout Game

PIERRE L'ENFANT designed the basic layout of our nation's capital. The plan featured 44 lettered streets and 52 numbered streets, as well as twenty avenues, totaling 228 miles of roads.

How would you lay out Washington if it were up to you? Is there a better layout for the city? How different would DC look with some other kind of plan, such as a straight grid like New York City? Since its creation, NYC's grid, called the "Randel Plan," has often been criticized as being too boring and uniform. People have accused it of destroying the city's natural character and geography.

But laying out a city isn't easy. One of the big concerns in urban planning is the ease of getting from one place to another. In this activity, you will try your hand at being an urban planner and laying out the streets and parks of Washington.

You'll Need
★ Floor or outdoor area with plenty of space
★ 30 feet of curling ribbon (from a party store)
★ 200 feet of curling ribbon in a different color
★ Scissors
★ Green construction paper
★ Toy car

The time is the early 1790s. Pierre L'Enfant is selected to map out the city's streets, but he becomes ill and they pick *you* instead. Now the fate of the city's layout is in your hands.

Before trying to draw it out on a piece of paper, you'll need to experiment on a larger scale. Lay the 30-foot ribbon on the floor or ground in a shape similar to the outline of Washington in the map on page 8.

Now cut the long ribbon into strips and lay them out to represent roads in your idea of a city layout. Use green construction paper to designate parks. Then attempt to navigate your car from one point to another within the "map." What is the best balance between an attractive layout and an efficiently navigable city?

I embrace with pleasure, and shall not delay my sanction to the plan when it shall have reached maturity."

The plan did not reach maturity until 1786, over 150 years later. John Carroll, the first Archbishop of Baltimore, at a meeting of the clergy, laid out a plan for a Catholic institution of higher learning and recommended a site. In 1787, a one-and-a-half-acre site was purchased in Georgetown for 75 pounds.

The Catholic Church sold some of its property to fund the building of the school, but it was not enough. A call for donations brought in some, but not that many. The first building was a modest three-story brick structure. In February 1790, Dr. Carroll admitted that "the fate of the school will depend much on the first impression made upon the public." Soon after that, something unexpected happened: Congress decided to locate the capital of the United States just minutes from Georgetown. Carroll was pleased, believing this would undoubtedly help his college gain popularity, and it did.

The new school first opened its doors to students in September 1791. The price of tuition was 10 pounds per year, which included books, paper, pens, ink, and firewood. The first boy to enroll was William Gaston of North Carolina, who later became a congressman. The second, Philemon Charles Wederstrandt, later com-

★ **Georgetown College in the 18th century.**

manded a fleet of ships. By the end of 1792, a total of 62 students had enrolled. It was not long before new land was acquired and new buildings built. The school was on its way to becoming one of the top universities in the nation.

A Capital Purchase

THE LAND that would make up the diamond-shaped District of Columbia was originally part of the states of Maryland and Virginia. Now it was under control of the federal government. These days, the city of Washington and the District of Columbia are one and the same. But back then, the capital city was a smaller area within the 10-square-mile federally controlled district; this was done intentionally so that the US capital would technically not be part of Maryland or Virginia or be dependent on those states for its protection. Aside from creating this buffer zone around Washington, the government initially didn't do anything with the DC land located outside of the capital city.

But as for the land that fell within the boundaries of Washington, the government would need it to build government buildings, to lay out streets and parks, and also to be able to offer land to citizens who wished to build homes and shops so the city could thrive. However, the land located within the city's boundaries had not been free for the taking. It previously belonged to 19 different landowners, and George Washington himself had negotiated with each of them to purchase their land.

The president had arrived at Georgetown from Philadelphia on March 28, 1791, after a one-week journey. On the morning of the 29th, a damp and misty day, he rode to the site of the capital city with the three commissioners and the two surveyors, Ellicott and L'Enfant, "but from the unfavorableness of the day, I derived no great satisfaction from the review." He met with the landowners, whose "fears and jealousies" were "counteracting the public purposes." Despite their initial hesitation, Washington, who was no doubt well known and respected by everyone present, managed to convince them. On March 30 the landowners signed an agreement and the deal was done.

It was a complicated deal at that. The owners received nothing for land that was to become streets, avenues, or parks. But they received $66.66 per acre of land that was to be used for public buildings—which amounted to a total of 541 acres (for a total of about $36,000). The remaining land was divided into building lots. The owners were to give half of those lots to the government, the sale of which would help pay for the construction of the city. The landowners were allowed to keep the other half of the lots for themselves, to build upon as they pleased.

The deal sounded OK to most of the landowners. They expected to make a profit even though they were required to donate some of

Survey the District Diamond

THE DISTRICT OF COLUMBIA was originally conceived as a diamond shape, 10 miles on each side. The boundaries of the diamond were set by Pierre L'Enfant's assistant, Andrew Ellicott. He began surveying the land using the 10-mile-by-10-mile diamond on February 12, 1791. The south cornerstone was the first placed, on April 15, 1791. Between 1791 and 1792, markers were placed at the other three points of the diamond, and then mile markers were placed along each side.

You'll Need
★ Photocopier, or computer with a scanner and printer
★ Ruler
★ Pencil or pen

In this activity, you will use a map of the Washington area to lay out the diamond and place the mile markers. Photocopy or scan/print the map on this page at its original size, and use the instructions below to plot out the District of Columbia diamond.

Begin at Jones Point, the small peninsula highlighted in gray at the bottom center of the map. From there, draw a line directly northwest into Virginia for 10 miles. You can use the compass rose in the lower right to determine the exact angle; the scale key in the lower left indicates that 1 mile equals 0.25 inches, so the line should be 10 × 0.25 inches, or 2.5 inches long. For the second side of the diamond, begin again at Jones Point and draw another line directly northeast across the Potomac into Maryland for 10 miles. For the third side, begin at the Virginia end of the first side and draw a line 10 miles directly northeast. For the final side, begin at the Maryland end of the second side and draw a line 10 miles directly northwest. If all your measurements line up, it should end at the same point as the third side, creating a diamond shape.

Interestingly, the District was not a precise diamond. The southwestern side was 10 miles 230.6 feet; the northeastern side 10 miles 263.1 feet; the southeastern side 10 miles 70.5 feet; and the northwestern side, 10 miles 63 feet.

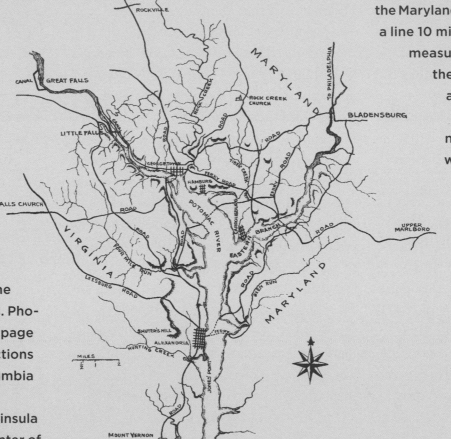

their land to the government, because the rest of their land was suddenly worth much more than it had been. And besides that, the terms of the agreement allowed them to continue using the land until such time as the government actually laid out streets and began to divide and sell lots.

A total of 10,136 building lots were acquired by the government. But there was not exactly a rush by the public to buy land in the future capital city. In fact, when the first auction of lots was held by the commissioners in George-town in October 1791, only 31 lots were sold. The government later sold 6,000 lots to real estate speculators James Greenleaf and Robert Morris in 1793 at a great discount. The terms of the sale required them to build 22 two-story brick houses per year, or, if they sold lots to others, the new owners would have to build at least one house per three lots sold. To help pay for their operations, Greenleaf and Morris borrowed $2 million from rich financiers in Holland. But the population increased slowly, and the lots they bought proved unprofitable. Greenleaf and Morris were unable to pay the commissioners or their creditors in Holland. By 1795, they had stopped building, and years of lawsuits followed.

The commissioners and the president asked Congress for permission to borrow money to help fund the construction of the public build-ings in the city. Congress gave its permission in 1796, and the commissioners were able to get a $200,000 loan from the state of Maryland, followed by another $50,000 in 1800.

But one of the original 19 landowners, David Burns, caused the government some trouble. Burns continued to farm his 500 acres (which included the land on which the White House currently sits) despite requests that his land was needed. Burns was upset that 17th Street would be constructed through his property and near his home, and that he'd not been given timely notice.

At one point in 1797, Burns became so an-gered that he published a notice in the news-paper that said, "I Hereby forewarn all persons from hunting with Dog or Gun, within my inclosures or any along my shores;—likewise, cutting down Timbers, Saplings, Bushes, of Wood of any kind, carrying off and burning Fence logs, any old wood on the shores; or in the woods;—If I should find any person tres-passing as above I will write to my attorney and suits will be commenced against the trespassers in the general court."

A few years later, Burns died, and the way was finally cleared for building to take place unhindered. Despite his reputation, Burns's daughter Marcia would become one of the most respected and beloved citizens of Wash-ington. She married a congressman who later became mayor of the city. When she died in 1832 at the age of 50 she was said to be the first American woman buried with public honors.

★ David Burns's cottage as seen in 1889.

Early Days

1792–1805

Planning the nation's capital was far easier on paper than in reality. When the ground was broken for the Capitol Building and the president's mansion, no one had any idea how long it would take to "finish" the city—or even to finish those two buildings.

The White House

PIERRE L'ENFANT's plans for the new capital city had envisioned a huge presidential palace. In March 1792, not long after L'Enfant was fired, the commissioners advertised in New York and Philadelphia newspapers for the design of "a President's House, to be erected in the city of Washington." The winner would receive $500.

More than a dozen plans were submitted. The winner of the competition was James Hoban, a young architect who had come to the United States from Ireland at the end of the Revolution, and had lived in Charleston, South Carolina, before moving to Washington. Hoban's design, both interior and exterior, were closely inspired by the Duke of Leinster's palace in Dublin, Ireland. Hoban impressed the commissioners so much that they not only accepted his plan and gave him the $500 but also gave him the personal authority to oversee construction of the President's House, at a large salary.

With President Washington and the commissioners in attendance, the cornerstone was laid on October 13, 1792. Hoban arranged to purchase sandstone for the exterior of the building from a quarry in Virginia. To protect it from weathering, the sandstone would be covered with white paint, which would eventually lead to it being called the White House.

In 1793, Hoban wanted to increase the size of the proposed building by 20 percent, but President Washington was not thrilled. He complained about the cost and said that it "would be best to take the plan on its original scale." In the end, Hoban's presidential residence was relatively small; it was only a quarter of the size of that proposed on L'Enfant's plans.

There were some delays in the construction when Congress refused to appropriate any further money for the construction of the mansion. Hoban left for New York, proclaiming he would not return, but President Washington got Congress to dedicate more money to the project, and Hoban came back to finish the project. After about two years, work finally resumed.

Sadly, President Washington never got the chance to live in the White House. His term as president ended in 1797, and construction was not completed until 1799. However, Washington stayed actively involved right up to the end of his life; he took a tour of the house a few weeks before his death on December 14, 1799.

Washington's successor, John Adams, was the first president to occupy the White House. When he and his family first lived there, only six of its rooms were furnished. The unfinished East Room contained piles of lumber and scaffolding, and First Lady Abigail Adams used it as a place to hang the wash for drying.

★ **James Hoban, on a stamp issued by the US Postal Service in 1981.** Author's collection

To some, the White House seemed too much like a king's palace rather than a president's home. At the time, Treasury Secretary Oliver Wolcott said, "It was built to be looked at by visitors and strangers, and will render its occupant an object of ridicule with some and of pity with others." But President Adams had lived in small, inconvenient houses in New York and Philadelphia since his inauguration as president in 1797, and he desired that his successors should be comfortably housed. Though he thought some of Hoban's ideas were extravagant, he allowed Hoban to finish what some critics of the time referred to as "the President's Palace."

Even when the mansion was finished, the grounds around the house were in a wild, rough state, and continued to be that way for many years after.

In the end, James Hoban became a permanent and well-respected resident of Washington, DC. He continued to design buildings, including several fine mansions and business structures, and became quite wealthy.

Building the Capitol

ONE OF Washington's most well-known and important buildings had a strange and complicated beginning. It all started in 1792, when a design contest for the Capitol Building—the place where Congress was to meet—was announced in newspapers around the country:

A premium of a lot in this city, to be designated by impartial judges, and $500, or a medal of that value, at the option of the party, will be given by the Commissioners of the Federal Buildings to the person who, before the 15th of July, 1792, shall produce to them the most approved plan for a capitol, to be erected in this city; and $250, or a gold medal, for the plan deemed next in merit to the one they shall adopt. The building to be of brick, and to contain the following apartments, to wit: A conference room and a room for the Representatives, sufficient to accommodate three hundred persons each; a lobby, or anteroom, to the latter; a Senate room of twelve hundred square feet area; an antechamber; twelve rooms of six hundred square feet each, for committee rooms and clerks' offices. It will be a recommendation of any plan if the central part of it may be detached and erected for the present with the appearance of a complete whole, and be capable of admitting the additional parts in future, if they shall be wanted. Drawings will be expected of the ground plots, elevations of each front, and sections through the building in such directions as may be necessary to explain the internal structure; and an estimate of the cubic feet of brick work composing the whole mass of the walls.

In response to this interesting advertisement, sixteen designs were submitted to the commissioners by architects from around the country. Secretary of State Thomas Jefferson himself had a great interest in architecture and had seen and admired some of Europe's finest public buildings. He was eager to be part of the process, hoping for a classical building that would be as impressive as the finest buildings in Europe.

Of the sixteen entries that were submitted, the winner was judged to be that of Dr. William Thornton of Pennsylvania, who was an amateur architect. Thornton's plan was considered to be the best of the lot, but it would need refinement by a professional.

To solve this problem, another entrant, a professional architect named William Hallett, who was an acquaintance of Pierre L'Enfant, was awarded second place, given $500, and was given the amateur Thornton's plan to put into effect. However, instead of refining the plans and making them suitable to build from, Hallett began to change them and make his own additions, to the dismay of the commissioners and President Washington, who had to ask him several times to finish the working drawings and not to make any changes to the design. The commissioners told him in strong words that they never said he was allowed to deviate from Thornton's plans. They asked him to write back and tell them he understood. Instead, Hallett gave his resignation, but it was not accepted. Hallett stopped working, refused to give up his drawings, and was then dismissed.

The north wing of the Capitol, to be built of freestone from the quarries of Aquia Creek, Virginia, was begun on September 18, 1793, with President Washington present at the laying of the cornerstone. A grand party followed the ceremony—a 500-pound ox was barbecued to feed the guests. In September 1793, James Hoban was made superintendent of the work at the Capitol, in addition to his assignment as architect and overseer of the White House.

In 1795, the work on the Capitol was taken over by George Hadfield. His design ideas were not embraced by the commissioners, and they dismissed him in 1798. At that point, James Hoban returned to overseeing construction of the Capitol, finishing the north wing in time for Congress to occupy it in 1800. Benjamin Latrobe was named architect of the Capitol in 1803, and he made significant contributions, completing the south wing and designing the reconstruction of the interior of the north wing.

From surveys of the future capital city, it had been decided that the hill in the eastern part of the city was the perfect location for the Capitol. It was built facing eastward, overlooking a two-mile plateau that was thought would be the site of the best houses. In the end, most of the city's growth ended up in the west, so the Capitol has its back facing the most populous part of the District of Columbia. The building was designated on L'Enfant's plan of the city as

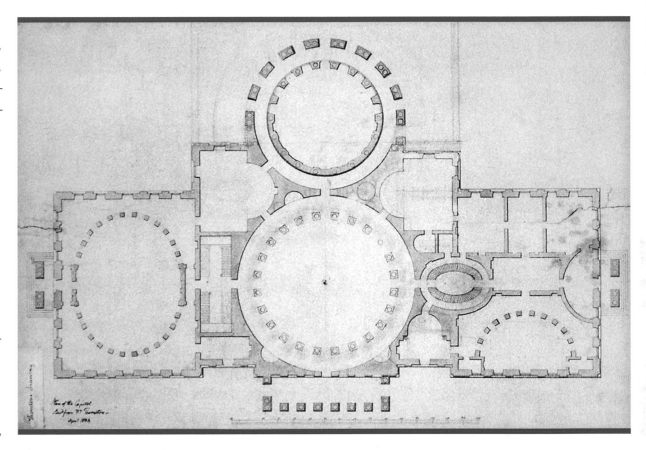

"The Capitol" and this name was adopted on the approval of President Washington.

★ **William Thornton's floor plan for the Capitol Building, 1793.**

Washington, DC, Under Construction

IT WAS indeed hard for anyone visiting the capital city in progress to visualize the finished product. There was a tremendous amount of work to be done, to basically make something out of nothing. Trees and bushes needed to be cut, ground had to be leveled, roads created, and government buildings, homes, and shops constructed. The future path of the great Pennsylvania Avenue was covered with bogs and marshes, insects, rabbits, and reptiles. Streams overflowed, causing a muddy mess. There were tangles of grapevines, thorn bushes, and blackberry vines.

A visitor named Thomas Twining wrote in 1796 of his visit to the site where the Capitol was being constructed, "The scene which surrounded me—the metropolis of a great nation in the first stage from sylvan state—was strikingly singular.... Looking from where I now stood I saw on every side a thick wood pierced with avenues in a more or less perfect state. These denoted the lines of the intended streets."

Another visitor wrote about what he saw during a visit to Washington in the late 1790s:

One wing of the Capitol only had been erected, which with the President's House, a mile distant, both constructed with white sandstone, were shining objects in dismal contrast with the scene around them. Instead of recognizing the avenues and streets portrayed in the plan of the city, not one was visible, unless we except a road with two buildings on each side of it, called the New Jersey Avenue. The Pennsylvania Avenue, leading, as laid down on paper, from the Capitol to the President's Mansion, was then nearly the whole distance a deep morass, covered with alder bushes.... Between the President's House and Georgetown a block of houses had been erected.... There were also two other blocks, consisting of two or three dwelling houses in different directions, and now and then an isolated wooden habitation; the intervening spaces, and indeed the surface of the city generally, being covered with shrub oak bushes on the higher grounds, and on the marshy soil with either trees or some sort of shrubbery.... The roads in every direction were muddy and unimproved. A sidewalk was attempted in one instance by a covering formed of the chips of the stones which had been hewed for the Capitol. It extended but a little way, and was of little value; for in dry weather the sharp fragments cut our shoes and in wet weather covered them with mortar.

The assistant postmaster held a more optimistic view. In June 1800, he wrote, "The situation of the city is extremely pleasant, and it will probably become the greatest city in America."

Open for Business

THE ORIGINAL plan was that the federal government would move to Washington on the first Monday in December 1800. In the spring of that year, Congress authorized the government's move to take place earlier. The president arrived in Washington on June 4, 1800, and Congress assembled there in November 1800.

The move cost about $40,000, and involved dozens of people and lots of furniture. The cost of packing and travel expenses for the people was about $24,000, while the cost of transportation for the furniture and papers was about $15,000. Packing up to move was a lot harder in those days. Carpenters had to be hired to make boxes, crates, and cases for the furniture and personal effects. One man kept an account of his expenses for the move to Washington, which included covering the carpenter's bill for board, paying for damage to his furniture along the way, the cost of obtaining a house in Washington, and the cost of living elsewhere until his house was ready.

President John Adams, in his speech at the opening of Congress on November 22, 1800, said, "I congratulate the people of the United States on the assembling of Congress at the permanent seat of their Government, and I congratulate you, gentlemen, on the prospect of a residence not to be changed.... You will consider it as the capital of a great nation, advancing with unexampled rapidity in arts, in commerce, in wealth, and in population; and possessing within itself those resources which, if not thrown away or lamentably misdirected, will secure to it a long course of prosperity and self-government."

Only the north wing of the Capitol was complete by the time Congress met, so both Senate and House met there.

Newspaper reporters and other writers in the early days of Washington had interesting ways of referring to the city. Some were admiring, others mocking. Among the names they used were Washington City, National Capital, Metropolis of the Country, Young Capital, New City of Washington, Palace in the Wilderness, First Born Child of the Union, Virgin Capital, Federal Seat, Capital of a New Nation, City of Magnificent Distances, Wide-spreading and Rural Metropolis, Washingtonople, the Capital of Miserable Huts, the Mud-hole, the City of Streets Without Houses, Beautiful Capital, Wilderness City, and Grand Emporium of the West. Abigail Adams herself called it a city only in name.

A businessman and diplomat named Benjamin Tayloe remembered, "I came to Washington in 1801, and remember it ... containing but a few thousand inhabitants scattered about in single houses apart from each other or in occasional groups, chiefly in the vicinity of the public buildings, from Georgetown to the Navy Yard. There was scarcely any pavement, except in front of detached houses."

Early Washington faced a definite housing shortage. There were too many people and not enough places to live. According to a letter by Abraham Bradley, Assistant Postmaster General, who arrived on May 29, "Provisions are plenty and cheap; but it will hardly be possible for all those attached to the public offices to be accommodated with houses within two miles of the offices."

There were also not enough public buildings ready to house all the government offices. The General Post Office (and the family of the assistant postmaster general) found temporary quarters in the three-story home of a Dr. Cracker at Ninth and E Streets NW, where not even half the rooms were finished when they moved in. The War Department leased a building on the south side of Pennsylvania Avenue owned by a man named Joseph Hodgson.

One visitor in 1804 wrote that "half starved cattle" were grazing among the bushes and that "quails and other birds are constantly shot within 100 yards of the Capitol during the sitting of Congress." When Irish poet Thomas Moore visited Washington in 1804, he wrote that the "embryo capital" was a place where "Fancy sees squares in morasses, obelisks in trees."

Back in 1793, there were 820 people living in Washington. By 1804, there were 4,352 residents, including 3,412 whites, 607 enslaved blacks, and 223 free blacks. In 1810, the population had increased to 8,208—ten times that of 1793.

Early DC Government

THOUGH WASHINGTON was the nation's capital and headquarters of our country's federal government, its citizens were not residents of any of the states, so they lost the right to vote in national elections after December 1, 1800.

As for the city itself—who was to run it? Between 1791 and 1801, government in the District of Columbia was run by the Corporations of Georgetown (incorporated 1789) and Alexandria (incorporated 1779), and by the three commissioners appointed by the president. These governing bodies were given the authority to lay out the future federal city, sell land to private buyers, and construct public buildings.

In 1801, a new system of local government was initiated, dividing DC into the County of Washington (which included territory acquired from Maryland) and the County of Alexandria

★ **This illustration was intended to show the view from the Capitol Building looking west in 1800, but it was drawn in 1834 and exaggerates Washington's appearance.**

(which included territory acquired from Virginia). Presidentially appointed justices of the peace ran the government within each county. Between 1802 and 1812, the mayor was appointed by the president. Between 1812 and 1820, the mayor was selected by the DC city council. In 1820, the people of DC won the right to elect their own mayor, and they continued to do so for the next 50 years, until the system was changed again (see page 78)

The first act passed by the city council authorized the creation of an official seal, which showed a building supported on 15 columns with the word "Washington" on top and "City Seal 1802" on the bottom.

Among other early acts passed by the council, one approved on October 6, 1802, regulated the size of bricks. It said that starting in January 1803, bricks sold in the city must be 8¾ inches long, 4¼ inches wide, and 2⅜ inches thick, and that they should be well burned. Anyone in Washington who made bricks that were smaller than that size would be fined $1 for every one thousand bricks. In August 1803, the Council approved spending $600 for erecting and repairing lamps in the city.

A Reluctant Mayor

UNDER THE first charter of the city, the mayor was appointed by the president of the United States. Thomas Jefferson, who became president in 1801, appointed a fifth-generation Virginian named Robert Brent, writing him a letter on June 3, 1802, asking if he would serve. Brent agreed. In 1806, Brent wrote that he "wished the president could have got some other person to execute the duties of this office" but since "it would be more agreeable to him, that I should continue to act, I am ready again to take upon myself the tasks, and will accept the commission accordingly."

In 1808, he wrote a letter in which he again indicated "my desire that some other person may be selected as Mayor in my place." By that time, Brent's plate was completely full. Not only was he mayor, he was also serving as a justice of the peace, a judge of the Orphan's Court, paymaster general of the army, and a member of the school board.

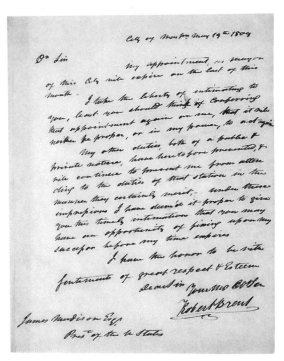

★ **Letter from Mayor Brent to the president, explaining his desire to step down.**

★ Famous Washingtonians ★

Many celebrities have been born in Washington, DC. The list includes: John F. Kennedy Jr., son of President John F. Kennedy, and Robert F. Kennedy Jr., son of Senator Robert F. Kennedy; longtime FBI director J. Edgar Hoover; Peter Tork of the 1960s pop music group the Monkees; actress Helen Hayes and actor William Hurt; actress Billie Burke, who played Glinda the Good Witch in *The Wizard of Oz*; actor Christopher Meloni, star of *Law & Order: Special Victims Unit*; comedian Louis C.K.; news anchor Connie Chung; Benjamin O. Davis, the country's first African American army general; Queen Noor of Jordan; civil rights activist Charles H. Houston; former vice president Al Gore; composer John Philip Sousa; and tennis player Pete Sampras.

Propose a Resolution

THOUSANDS OF NEW LAWS are proposed every year in Congress, by lawmakers from all over the country. During the 113th Congress, 2013–2014, a total of 5,884 bills and resolutions were introduced in the House, and another 3,020 were put before the Senate!

Some resolutions simply express the opinion of the House or the Senate—for example, to recognize the anniversary of a historic event or the contributions of a person or a certain group of people. A *simple resolution* expresses the opinion of one chamber of Congress, and a *concurrent resolution* expresses the opinion of both chambers, Senate and House. A *joint resolution*, however, is one that proposes legislation and requires the approval of the president.

In this activity, you'll draft your own simple resolution. What event, holiday, person or persons would you like to have officially recognized? Remember that what you are proposing to be recognized by Congress must have national significance and apply to the whole country. Look at the following text from an actual resolution introduced during the 114th Congress as an example.

H.RES.115
114th CONGRESS, 1st Session
February 13, 2015

RESOLUTION
Recognizing the cultural and historical significance of Lunar New Year.

Whereas Lunar New Year begins on the second new moon following the winter solstice, or the first day of the new year according to the lunisolar calendar, and extends until the full moon 15 days later;

Whereas the 15th day of the new year, according to the lunisolar calendar, is called the Lantern Festival;

Whereas Lunar New Year is often referred to as "Spring Festival" in various Asian countries;

Whereas many religious and ethnic communities use lunar-based calendars;

Whereas Lunar New Year began in China more than 4,000 years ago and is widely celebrated in East and Southeast Asia;

Whereas the Asian diaspora has expanded the Lunar New Year celebration into an annual worldwide event;

Whereas Lunar New Year is celebrated by millions of Asian Americans, and by many non-Asian Americans, in the United States;

Whereas Lunar New Year is celebrated with community activities and cultural performances;

Whereas participants celebrating Lunar New Year travel to spend the holiday reuniting with family and friends; and

Whereas Lunar New Year is traditionally a time to wish upon others good fortune, health, prosperity, and happiness: Now, therefore, be it

Resolved, *That the House of Representatives—*

(1) recognizes the cultural and historical significance of Lunar New Year;

(2) in observance of Lunar New Year, expresses its deepest respect for Asian Americans and all individuals throughout the world who celebrate this significant occasion; and

(3) wishes Asian Americans and all individuals who observe this holiday a happy and prosperous new year.

Brent was reappointed nine times, several times accepting under protest. In 1812, after 10 years in office, he finally refused to serve again.

Water, Water, Everywhere

In 1807 nearly the whole lower part of what is now the Mall was wet, marshy ground covered with reeds. Logs were piled into mud holes to make them passable. Besides streams and creeks and marshes, the city was rich in springs. By L'Enfant's estimation, there were more than 25 springs within the boundaries of the future city. (In fact, there were probably over 35 of them.) In the early days of Washington, some of these springs were used to supply water to the residents. One spring located on a nearby farm was for a time used to supply water to the Capitol.

As with any growing city, as the population increased and more buildings were built, these springs were filled in, and water had to be supplied from other sources, including the Potomac River.

Fire!

One of young city's first fires destroyed the War Department building and its neighboring building on November 8, 1800. Another great fire occurred on January 20, 1801, at the

★ A Famous Hotel ★

Blodgett's Hotel was designed by James Hoban and completed in 1793. In 1810, it was purchased by the US government to house the patent office and general post office. Congress met there after Washington, DC, was burned by the British, until the Capitol was rebuilt.

★ **Blodgett's Hotel.**

Treasury Department. It was extinguished by citizens using water buckets, but not until after several valuable books had been destroyed. These two fires quickly demonstrated that protection against fire had to be taken seriously.

A city law enacted in 1803 said homeowners or business proprietors must buy at their own expense as many 2.5-gallon leather fire buckets as there were stories to their building. The penalty for failing to do so was $1 per missing bucket. The same law also said that the city would obtain a fire engine, to be kept neat the Center Market. Soon after, two more fire engines were added. In 1804, the city was divided into four fire wards, each one having a fire company.

Washington Burns

1805-1840

Though the population of Washington grew steadily in its first decades, the city still could not compare to New York, Philadelphia, or Boston. The capital had a huge setback in 1814, when the British invaded and burned most of the government buildings in the city.

Washington's Early Bridges

Because Washington was surrounded by rivers and creeks, building bridges was an important step in helping people and goods move into and out of the city. The first bridge to be built in what is now Washington spanned Rock Creek, between Washington and Georgetown. It was erected in 1788, at about where M Street stands today. Another bridge, a three-arched stone bridge, was built at the site of K Street in 1792. President Adams crossed the K Street bridge when he moved into Washington in 1800. This bridge, which was built out of stone leftover from the construction of the capital's first government buildings, stood until 1869.

During most of the 18th century, the Potomac could be crossed only by ferry. Finally, in 1797, a wooden covered bridge at Little Falls became the first Potomac crossing. It was a toll bridge, and the fee was 3 cents for a pedestrian and 25 cents for a two-wheeled vehicle. The bridge rotted to pieces by 1804; it was replaced but the replacement was destroyed by flooding soon after.

The next bridge in the city was the 136-foot-long stone and iron Chain Bridge, built at Little Falls in 1810. Tolls ranged from 6½ cents for a pedestrian to 37½ cents for a two-horse wagon to $1.50 for a four-horse carriage. This bridge did not last long, either, destroyed by flooding in 1812. The fourth and fifth bridges at that site were also damaged by floods, as was the sixth bridge, built in the 1850s. A seventh Little Falls Bridge was built in 1874, and was damaged by flooding in 1936. The eighth Chain Bridge was built in 1939.

Meanwhile, in 1809, Long Bridge was built at 14th Street by the Washington Bridge Company. The toll for this mile-long draw bridge ranged from 3 cents for animals to $1 for stagecoaches. The bridge was destroyed in 1814, during the War of 1812—the retreating Americans burned the Virginia side to prevent the British from crossing, and the British simultaneously burned the Washington end to stop the Americans from getting into Washington. But within a few years, the bridge was rebuilt. It was damaged by flooding and ice in 1831, and the government had a new one erected in 1835. Ice and water damage plagued the bridge over the years that followed.

The quarter-mile-long Aqueduct Bridge was built between 1833 and 1843. This bridge was a canal bridge, built to carry boats from the Chesapeake and Ohio Canal in Georgetown to the Alexandria Canal across the Potomac River. The bridge was an engineering feat—it was built on eight stone piers that extended 36 feet under the water. The piers were built under the water with the help of *cofferdams*, giant wooden barrels that extended from the river's surface all the way down to the riverbed.

Once the cofferdams were in place, the water could be pumped out of them, allowing the builders to stay dry even as they worked at the bottom of the river.

A crossing for the Anacostia River was chartered by the state of Maryland in 1795, and the 20-foot-wide bridge at Pennsylvania Avenue SE was completed in 1804. Like the Long Bridge, it was burned by the Americans during the British invasion of 1814 to prevent the British from reaching the capital. A replacement bridge caught fire from steamboat sparks in

1845, and a new replacement was not built until decades later.

Washington Burns

JUST 30 years after the Revolution, America and Great Britain found themselves in conflict again, over issues such as Britain's trade restrictions, and their differences escalated into another war. The War of 1812 was fought widely, in such places as Michigan, Illinois, Indiana, and Missouri—which at the time were US

★ **The Chain Bridge as seen in the early 19th century.**

territories, not yet states—as well as Canada, Ohio, New York, and Maryland.

On April 28, 1813, American forces captured the fort and town of York in Upper Canada, the site of present-day Toronto. The troops looted, burned, and vandalized much of the city, prompting an outcry from the British government—and a call for revenge.

The next year, Britain was able to turn its full military attention to the United States, after having defeated the French emperor Napoleon Bonaparte at Waterloo. Thousands of British troops sailed from Bermuda to Maryland in August 1814, with their sights on the nation's capital.

By Monday, August 22, much of Washington was abandoned as word spread of the impending arrival of the British. American forces assembled to the northeast of the capital to try to prevent the British from advancing. They gathered an impressive total of 7,000, but only 500 of them were full-time trained soldiers, the rest being militia. The British were outnumbered but had superior, better-trained forces. The battle that took place on August 24 at Bladensburg, Maryland, about five miles from Washington, was a short one. By around 4 PM, the Americans had been defeated, beating a hasty retreat. After a short rest, the British army began their march toward Washington.

Meanwhile, Washingtonians continued to leave their city in droves, anticipating what was going to happen next. By the afternoon of the 24th, only a brave few remained behind, and the nation's capital was mostly a ghost town. General William Winder, who led the retreating Americans, considered leaving some troops behind in Washington to try to hold off the British, but it appeared to be a lost cause, so they all fled, leaving the nation's capital unprotected.

President James Madison himself had already left, and the President's House was mostly empty, except for First Lady Dolley Madison and some of her staff. Mrs. Madison had personally collected documents and some keepsakes and had them loaded into a wagon. She hoped for the best and told the servants to continue preparing for the usual gathering of the president and his cabinet. Even after Bladensburg and the retreat of American troops through Washington toward the west, Mrs. Madison remained dedicated to one last goal: safely removing a now famous life-size portrait of George Washington that had been painted by Gilbert Stuart.

In a letter written to her sister as the Battle of Bladensburg raged, Mrs. Madison wrote, "Will you believe it, my sister? We have had a battle, or skirmish, near Bladensburg, and here I am still, within sound of the cannon! Mr. Madison comes not. May God protect us! Two messengers, covered with dust, come to bid me fly; but here I mean to wait for him.... At this late hour a wagon has been procured, and I have had it filled with plate and the most valuable portable articles, belonging to the house. Whether it will reach its destination, the 'Bank of Maryland,' or fall into the hands of British soldiery, events must determine. Our kind friend, Mr. Carroll, has come to hasten my departure, and in a very bad humor with me, because I insist on waiting until the large picture of General Washington is secured, and it requires to be unscrewed from the wall. This process was found too tedious for these perilous moments; I have ordered the frame to be broken, and the canvas taken out. It is done! and the precious portrait placed in the hands of two gentlemen of New York, for safe keeping."

Finally, she departed, and just in time too, because the British were closing in. At around 8 o'clock that evening, British forces under the command of Vice Admiral Sir Alexander Cockburn and Major General Robert Ross reached Washington. Still upset over the destruction of York, the British had vengeance on their minds. This was just the opportunity they were seeking. They planned to burn all the government buildings in Washington but spare private property if they could.

The secretary of the navy told Commodore Thomas Tingey that if the Americans lost at Bladensburg, he was to destroy whatever he could of the Navy Yard rather than let it fall into enemy hands. At 8:20 PM, Commodore Tingey set fire to the 10-gun sloop of war *Argus*, the frigate *Columbia*, and a large quantity of naval stores. The Americans also destroyed two bridges.

The newly arrived British headed straight for the Capitol. From the direction they came it was the first public building they would encounter. As General Ross was riding along, his horse was shot by a sniper in a nearby home. His troops burned the house, and then they marched to the Capitol and fired rockets into its windows. Then they entered the building, and went into the House Chamber. Ross and Cockburn headed to the Speaker's chair and yelled out, "Shall this harbor of Yankee Democracy be burned? All for it say aye!" The response was overwhelming: the soldiers shouted, "Fire the building!" The troops searched around and collected whatever flammable material they could find, including books and papers from the Congressional Library, stacked it up on the floor of the House, and placed a lit torch to the piles.

After starting the fire in the Capitol, the troops marched up Pennsylvania Avenue and set fire to the other government buildings. They took possession of a lodging house belonging to a woman named Mrs. Suter and demanded dinner. They entered the President's House and found the dining room table set for 40 guests, just as Mrs. Madison had directed. There were bottles of wine chilling, and meat was on the spits in the kitchen. Ross and Cockburn did not eat anything at the President's House, but the men took a few souvenirs before setting the mansion afire and returning to Mrs. Suter's. They extinguished the candles and ate their dinner by the light of the burning buildings. They set fire to the Treasury Building and the State, War, and Navy Departments. Dr. William Thornton, who had originally designed the Capitol and was now the US government's superintendent of patents, convinced the British not to torch the Patent Office, since it contained the records of inventions that belonged to private citizens. All told, the invaders caused over $1.2 million in damage.

It was a scary time for the few who had stayed behind. One of them was a woman named Mrs. Vernon, whose husband, a militia captain, had marched off to Bladensburg that morning but had not returned. Mrs. Vernon had an infant in her arms and sat with her neighbor, a Mrs. Bender, who came in "frightened almost out of her wits, with a bottle of camphor in one hand and a handkerchief in the other."

About 200 British soldiers proceeded to the Navy Yard to complete the destruction that had been started by the Americans. They threw a torch into a pit where the Americans had hidden kegs of gunpowder for safekeeping, resulting in a huge explosion. According to an eyewitness, "Large pieces of earth, stones, bricks, shot, shells, etc., burst into the air, and, falling among us (who had nowhere to run, being on a narrow neck of land, with the sea on three sides), killed about twelve men and wounded above thirty more, most of them in a dreadful manner." In fact, this witness underestimated the death toll; almost 100 British soldiers were killed or wounded in the explosion.

Meanwhile, more destruction was in store for the young city. On August 25, just one day after the attack, a huge and fierce thunderstorm hit Washington. Dark skies, lightning, pounding rain, and terrible winds caused major damage. The heavy rain helped to douse some of the fires that had been set the day before, but a tornado ripped trees from the ground and destroyed many homes. According to one of the British invaders, "Roofs of houses were

★ **The burning of Washington in 1814.**

torn off and carried up into the air like sheets of paper. . . . This lasted for two hours without intermission, during which time many of the houses spared by us were blown down, and thirty of our men, with as many more of the inhabitants, were buried beneath the ruins. Two cannons standing upon a bit of rising ground were fairly lifted in the air and carried several yards to the rear."

The office of the *National Intelligencer*, an anti-British newspaper, was raided. British soldiers destroyed the presses and burned the archive of past issues. Other private property destroyed included a hotel built by Daniel Carroll, a house that had been built for George Washington near Capitol Hill, and a rope factory located near the Navy Yard.

The British did not stay long. They decided to abandon Washington on the 25th, before the Americans could muster a counterattack. That night, they began to quietly leave the city. "It was about eight o'clock at night," according to an eyewitness, "that a staff officer, arriving on the ground, gave directions for the corps to form in marching order. Preparatory to this step large quantities of fresh fuel were heaped upon the fires, while from every company a few men were selected, who should remain beside them till the pickets withdrew, and move about from time to time so that their figures might be seen by the light of the blaze. After this the troops stole to the rear of the fires by

★ *He Slept in the Forest* ★

President Madison had fled to Virginia on August 24. Upon hearing that the British were advancing even farther, he retreated into the forest. Though the news turned out to be false, the president spent the night of the 25th in a forester's hut.

twos and threes; when far enough removed to avoid observation, they took their places and in profound silence began their march. The night was very dark. . . . We moved on, however, in good order. No man spoke above his breath, our steps were planted lightly, and we cleared the town without exciting observation."

★ **The severely damaged Capitol Building after it was burned by the British (the Capitol dome had not yet been built).**

Rebuilding the Capital

WHEN THE citizens of Washington returned, they were aghast at the destruction. Some of their homes had been damaged or destroyed by the storm, and the public buildings that symbolized their nation had been devastated. Their unfinished capital city had suffered a serious setback. Critics took up the cause of relocating the capital elsewhere.

When Congress met again in September, they used the Patent Office as their temporary headquarters. A measure was introduced in the House of Representatives to move the capital to Philadelphia, at least temporarily. The vote was close, 83 to 74, but Washington was to remain the capital city.

Upon returning to Washington on August 27, President Madison looked over the ruins of his former home, and then moved his family into a building called the Octagon House on the northeast corner of New York Avenue and 18th Street. The Madisons spent that winter there, and in February 1815, in the second floor study, the president added his signature to the Treaty of Ghent, the agreement with Britain that ended the War of 1812. The Madisons paid $500 in rent to the owners of Octagon House, which had been designed by Dr. William Thornton (original architect of the Capitol) and completed in 1800.

The president and his family later moved to the northwest corner of Pennsylvania Avenue and 19th Street, where they lived for the remainder of his term.

James Hoban, the presidential mansion's original architect, was called in to reconstruct it. Though the exterior walls were still stand-

★ **The Octagon House can still be visited today; it is operated as a museum by the American Institute of Architects.**

The Octagon
museum

AMERICAN ARCHITECTURAL FOUNDATION
AMERICAN INSTITUTE OF ARCHITECTS

ing, they were damaged by the heat and had to be demolished. The reconstruction, basically a complete rebuild, took three years; President James Monroe was its first new inhabitant.

The Treasury Building and Navy Yard were rebuilt relatively quickly, but the reconstruction of the Capitol Building was a more complex process. Capitol architect Benjamin Latrobe, who in 1814 was busy working with inventor Robert Fulton on the design and construction of a steamboat, was called back to Washington to work on it. Disagreements with the commissioner of public buildings and later with the new president, James Monroe, led Latrobe to resign in 1817. His successor was Thomas Bullfinch, who saw the Capitol to its completion, not only rebuilding the two damaged wings but also finishing the central portion and capping it with a stone-and-wood dome. By the late 1820s his work was done.

A Growing City

WITH ITS most prominent buildings reconstructed, and its place as the nation's permanent capital no longer in question, the city of Washington continued to grow and thrive. As the nation grew, so did the federal government, and that contributed to the city's expansion.

The cornerstone of the new city hall building was laid in 1820 with great ceremony. At that time there were 2,028 houses and 129 shops and other buildings. By the end of 1829, the total was 3,061 houses and 259 shops; by 1839 there were 3,956 houses and 432 shops; and by the end of the 1840s the number had climbed to 6,323 houses and 580 shops. The first four-story building was built in 1850, and by 1853, 64 four-story buildings had been built.

Even by the 1830s, many lots of land had yet to be sold. Street improvements were slow to

★ **Washington in 1834.**

Create a Watermark

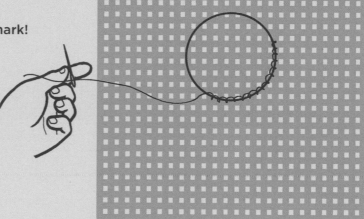

THOUGH THE US MINT is headquartered in Washington, no coins are minted there. The Bureau of Engraving and Printing, which is responsible for our paper money, does print money in Washington, DC (as well as in Fort Worth, Texas). In 2014 alone, the bureau printed more than 2.2 billion one-dollar bills, 563 million five-dollar bills, 486 million 10-dollar bills, and 1.7 billion 20-dollar bills.

Counterfeiting—the illegal practice of creating fake bills in the hopes of passing them off as real money—has been an issue for many years, but in the past it could only be attempted by someone who could afford to buy expensive equipment. With the advent of high-quality, low-cost printers and scanners, the government has had to take measures to prevent the average criminal from printing money. Security features on our paper money today include a special thread running through the bill, holograms, and a *watermark*.

What is a watermark? It is an area on a paper bill that is slightly thinner than the rest of the bill, creating a design that can only be seen when held up to the light. A similar watermark effect can be created with a computer graphics or word processing program by placing a faint image in the background of a printed design, but a *true* watermark—one that responds to light—can only be made during the papermaking process.

Try your hand at making a watermark!

You'll Need

★ A papermaking kit that includes a screen

★ Twist ties made from paper and wire (the type that come with some packaged foods— the longer the better) or a roll of thin, flexible metal wire

★ Needle and thread

★ Toothpicks (optional)

If you are using a twist tie, twist the paper so it wraps tightly around the wire. (Or very carefully remove the paper from the wire, leaving only the wire. Be careful; it's sharp!)

What design do you want to create as a watermark on your paper? You could make a simple circle, a triangle, a letter shape, or any shape that you can create by bending the wire. If you are using wire from a roll, you have more length to play with and could use a cookie cutter as a guide, wrapping the wire around it into that cookie cutter shape. When you have decided what to create, make the shape and carefully sew it onto the screen as shown, making sure it is secure and does not move when you hold the screen up. You could also use toothpicks to make a geometric design, sewing them onto the screen instead of the wire.

Once you've done that, you are all set to make your watermarked paper. Follow the papermaking kit instructions, with the screen design-side up . . . and when the paper dries and you peel it off the screen, you should be able to see your watermark.

come. Pennsylvania Avenue was by far in the best condition of all the city's streets, and even it had yet to be paved.

As the population grew, so did the number of churches in the young city. The First Baptist Church was completed in 1809, the Second Baptist Church in 1810, St. Patrick's Church in 1810, St. Peter's at Capitol Hill in 1821, and St. John's Episcopal in 1816. Christ Church at the Navy Yard was built in 1807, and until St. John's was built it was the only Episcopal church in the city; both Jefferson and Madison attended services there. Once St. John's was completed in 1816, it was frequented by a long line of presidents beginning with Madison. During renovations to the church in 1883, President Chester Arthur donated a stained glass window in memory of his wife, who had died before he took office. Arthur asked that the window be installed on the south side of the church so he could see it from the window of his White House study.

Before long, Washington became quite the society city. It was home to hundreds of wealthy American politicians, as well as foreign diplomats, and there were numerous balls and elegant dinner parties held throughout the year. By 1810, Washington had overtaken Georgetown as the social center of the area. These parties featured a mixture of Washington's high society, government officials, and honored guests such as Marquis de Lafayette, a French military leader who fought for the United States in the American Revolution. Lafayette visited the capital in 1824–25, and many parties were thrown in his honor.

Washington had some interesting laws in the 1820s. For example, anyone racing a horse on the streets of Washington within 300 yards of someone's home would be fined $10. Hogs were not allowed south of Massachusetts Avenue or they would be seized and sold at auction. Shooting off firecrackers within 200 yards of a house would mean a $5 fine.

By 1829 there were nine banks located within the District of Columbia, three of which were in Washington City: the Bank of Washington, the Bank of the Metropolis, and the Patriotic Bank of Washington. Pennsylvania Avenue was home to a good variety of stores selling everything from groceries to hardware to hats.

★ Billiard Brouhaha ★

When word leaked that President John Quincy Adams had a billiard table installed in the White House in 1825, his opponents seized on this to ridicule him and try to prevent his reelection in 1828. It was seen as scandalous that a president would play such a game. In addition, though the president got the table used and it cost only $50, the Washington newspaper *United States Telegraph* reported it had cost $500. Complaints about the cost of the table were unjustified, since the president's son had paid for it from his own pocket. Adams did not win reelection, though it is highly unlikely that the billiards "scandal" had much to do with that.

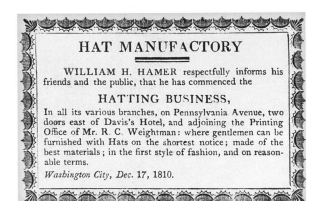

★ **Ad for a Washington hatter, 1810.**

In 1830 there were two free schools in Washington, one in the east and one in the west, with a combined total of 400 children.

Lafayette Square

LOCATED JUST north of the White House, Lafayette Square was part of the White House grounds until 1804. In fact, it was used to store construction material during the building of the president's home. Originally known as Presidents Park, in 1824 this seven-acre space was renamed in honor of Revolutionary War hero Marquis de Lafayette.

The neighborhood surrounding the park was one of 19th-century Washington's most prestigious. The first building on the square was St. John's Church in 1816. Elegant Federal-style houses followed, and before long, it was a highly sought-after location. The first house was the Decatur House, built in 1819. After the death of its first owner, Commodore Stephen Decatur, it housed in succession three different British ministers, a Russian minister, future president Martin Van Buren when he was secretary of state, and Vice President George Dallas, elected with President James K. Polk in 1844.

★ **St. John's Church in Lafayette Square, circa 1920.**

Supreme Court Scrapbook

THE SUPREME COURT is constantly in the news, especially when it is hearing oral arguments. Some cases are instant landmarks, others are soon forgotten, and still others may grow in stature over time. In this activity you will keep a Supreme Court–related scrapbook.

You'll Need
- ★ 2 newspapers
- ★ 2 newsmagazines
- ★ Scissors
- ★ Glue stick
- ★ Empty scrapbook or notebook

Peruse at least two newspapers and two magazines over at least a one-month period for any stories pertaining to the Supreme Court. (For better results, look for stories over a two- or three- month period or longer, between October and June, which is when the Supreme Court is in session.) Cut out the articles you find. Paste them neatly and chronologically into a scrapbook, labeling each one at the top with the date and publication. When you are done, you will have a nice record of the cases and controversies of the Supreme Court. What themes emerge?

Other notable residents who lived on the square included Secretary of State William Henry Seward, who served under Lincoln, and South Carolina senator John C. Calhoun. The Blair House, built 1824, served as home for Harry S. Truman while the White House was being renovated in 1948–1952.

The park was formally landscaped in 1851.

George Washington University

GEORGE WASHINGTON'S will left money designated toward the founding of an institution of higher learning in the nation's capital, but it would be more than 20 years before his vision became a reality. With the assistance of President James Monroe, 32 members of Congress, and a reverend named Luther Rice, a college was finally founded. On February 9, 1821, Monroe signed the Act of Congress that created the Columbian College in the District of Columbia.

When it first opened in 1821, the school had three professors, one tutor, and 30 students located in a single building. Its initial location was between 14th and 15th Streets, a 30-minute walk west of the Capitol. Early subjects included English, Latin, Greek, mathematics, chemistry, astronomy, and navigation. The first class graduated in 1824. Not long after, a medical school and a law school were added. By 1830, the college had eight professors and the school library had 4,000 books.

In 1873, the name changed from Columbian College to Columbian University and moved to 15th and L Streets. The school now allowed women to enroll, and began to offer doctoral degrees. The name changed to George Washington University in 1904, and in 1912 it moved to its present location in Foggy Bottom.

Bicycle Rider Causes Spectacle

ONE OF the very first American sightings of a *velocipede*, an early form of the bicycle, happened on Pennsylvania Avenue in 1827. A foreign diplomat appeared on the street riding one of these odd-looking contraptions with no pedals, which had been imported from London. Crowds gathered to witness this bizarre demonstration. It was quite a sight to see the gentleman pushing himself over the rough, uneven dirt terrain, one foot after the other.

According to a 19th-century account, "He held the handle bars with firm grasp of both hands, and with head erect looked straight to the front from the eye sockets. As the story goes, he was dressed in knee-breeches, with buckles and pumps, dress coat, ruffled shirt, and a high silk hat pressed closely down to his ears. In profile the gallant velocipedist exhibited a picturesque personation of an amateur athlete standing on tiptoe astraddle two wheels on parade before a multitude gaping with surprise and wonderment."

Inaugurations

THE NATION's first president, George Washington, had been inaugurated first in New York and then, for his second term, in Philadelphia, which was then the capital city. John Adams was inaugurated in Philadelphia in 1797 and began his four-year term there, but moved to Washington in 1800. Later that year, Adams lost his bid for reelection to Thomas Jefferson, who became the first president to be inaugurated in the new capital.

On March 4, 1801, Jefferson rode his horse "Wildair" unescorted along muddy Pennsylvania Avenue, greeting those who waved to him along the way. When he got to the Capitol Building, he hitched his horse to a fence along the western edge of the grounds and made his way quite casually inside and into the Senate Chamber, where he delivered his inaugural address. After Chief Justice John Marshall administered the oath of office to him, he went back outside, got on his horse, and rode to the White House, where he held a reception to celebrate his inauguration.

In 1817, James Monroe was the first to be inaugurated outdoors, on the eastern portico of the Capitol. At his next inauguration, the

★ *Washington A-to-Z in 1822* ★

The 1822 City Directory lists over 1,500 of the city's residents along with their occupation and address. Here is an A-to-Z sampler of some of the folks you might have encountered in early 19th century Washington:

Giovanni Andrei, chief carver at the Capitol

John Bailey, letter carrier and assistant clerk in the city post office

Overton Carr, cashier at the Patriotic Bank

Catharine Davis, widow

John Ellis, candlemaker

Lewis Fronk, glassblower

Samuel Gardner, dyer

James Hanna, stone cutter

Phillip Inch, painter

Matthias Jeffers, plasterer

Thomas Keatly, ship carpenter

John Latruit, watchmaker and jeweler

Jane Marr, tavernkeeper

James Neale, professor of mathematics at Catholic Seminary

John Orr, gardener

Pennell Palmer, hat store proprietor

John Queen, master bricklayer at the Capitol

Daniel Rapine, bookseller

Carey Selden, coal merchant

Charles Thompson, wood merchant

John Underwood, clerk at the first auditor's office, treasury department

Charles Varden, coach maker

Zachariah Walker, pump maker

David Young, butcher

weather was deemed too cold for an outdoor ceremony, so it was held inside, as was that of the next president, John Quincy Adams. When Andrew Jackson took office, the ceremony was once again moved outdoors to the Capitol's eastern portico (where it has been held ever since). Like Jefferson, Jackson rode his horse unescorted along Pennsylvania Avenue, and was cheered wildly by the crowds that had gathered, some coming from as far as 500 miles away to see the war hero on his way to becoming president. The next president, Martin Van Buren, rode with his predecessor to the Capitol on March 4, 1837, in a fine carriage pulled by four horses. Next came William Henry Harrison, another war hero, who was accompanied by a military escort including a battalion of his former soldiers.

As the years passed, the crowds became bigger and the parties more numerous. At Grover Cleveland's inauguration in 1885, the crowd was estimated to be between 150,000 and 200,000 people, the parade included 30,000 men in uniform, and Pennsylvania Avenue was colorfully decked out with all kinds of flags and banners. In 2009, a crowd of 1.8 million people turned out for Barack Obama's first inauguration.

Canal Schemes

PIERRE L'ENFANT'S original plan for the city included a canal that ran from the Potomac River at what is now Foggy Bottom, west to east through the heart of the city, then veered south at the Capitol and split into two branches, one leading back to the Potomac and the other to the Eastern Branch.

George Washington liked this idea, and even after Ellicott reimagined L'Enfant's plan, the canal was still a part of it. Not only would it be pleasant to look at, but a canal would also help move goods into and around the city. Construction of the canal, however, would be costly, and it was not funded by the government. In 1802, Congress gave the Washington Canal Company a charter, allowing them to raise money to dig the canal. Part of the canal was what used to be Tiber Creek. A groundbreaking ceremony was held in 1810, but the company soon ran out of money. Miraculously, they managed to raise $47,000 and complete the work on the canal by the end of 1815. Unfortunately, the tides caused

★ **Andrew Jackson's entourage heads to the White House during his second inauguration in 1829.**

problems and the canal needed more work to make it usable.

Meanwhile, the Chesapeake and Ohio Canal from Georgetown to the Ohio River was approved by Congress in 1825, and ground was broken in 1828.

Progress on the Washington Canal was slow. The city of Washington took over control of the Washington Canal Company in 1832, and passed a law stating what improvements needed to be made—widening, extending, repairing—and granting the right to collect tolls, so long as the required improvements had been made first. Though in theory, this canal could have been a very useful addition to the city, it never quite worked out that way. With the introduction of the railroad into Washington in the mid-19th century, the canal became even less important.

It was not long before the canal became an open sewer, filled with filth and difficult to navigate. In 1855, the city allocated $2,500 for improving the canal, but it just wasn't enough. The canal was eventually abandoned, and in 1873, $65,000 was spent on filling it in.

★ *Too Many Reps?* ★

In an 1832 letter to one of his constituents, Congressman Peter Ihrie from Pennsylvania talked about the rule regulating apportionment, or how the population of a state would determine its number of members in the House of Representatives. At that time, he explained, there was a law proposed that would fix the number of people per representative at 48,000. This system was discontinued in the 20th century, and in 1929 the size of the House was capped at 435 representatives. Thank goodness for that, because if the ratio had stayed at one representative for every 48,000 people, the House of Representatives today would have more than 6,500 members!

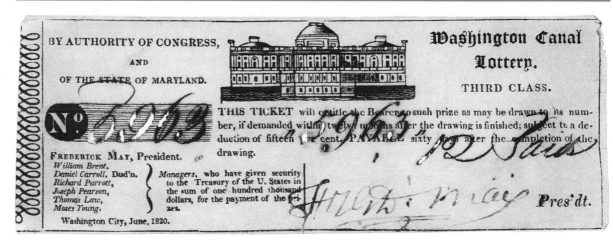

 A canal lottery was held in 1820 to raise money for the completion of the Washington Canal.

★ ★ ★

Three Landmarks

4

1840-1860

The mid-19th century was a time of growth, change, and unrest for Washington. During these years, the city saw three major construction projects: the Capitol was expanded and its dome replaced, the Washington Monument was started, and the first building of the Smithsonian Institution was built. All were important landmarks that forever changed the appearance of the city.

The *Princeton* Disaster

ON FEBRUARY 28, 1844, an impressive new warship made its public debut on the Potomac River. As a crowd watched from the banks of the river, the ship's captain, Robert Stockton, fired the *Princeton*'s two massive cannons at some ice floes. These cannons, the largest shipboard cannons ever made (the "Oregon" weighed 7 tons and the "Peacemaker" 10 tons) were able to fire a 213-pound ball up to 3 miles.

A little while later, more than 500 government officials and prominent Washington residents, including President John Tyler and 79-year-old former First Lady Dolley Madison, boarded the impressive 954-ton warship for a dinner party and demonstration.

The ship, which had anchored near Alexandria, was the navy's first screw-propeller steamship. As part of the festivities, it sailed a short distance down the river. On the return trip, one of the government officials on board asked Captain Robert Stockton to fire the 12-inch cast-iron cannon called "Peacemaker" once more for another up-close demonstration of the gun's mighty firepower. Stockton had intended to be done with the guns for the day, but he agreed to do it anyway.

What happened next was described by the gunner who loaded the cannon: "After the ship had been put about on her return up the river, a request was made by some of the gentlemen on board that the gun might be fired again; which request I had conveyed to Captain Stockton, and received from him orders to load the gun as had been done in the two previous discharges, with 25 lbs. of powder, and one shot of about 212 lbs."

Most of the female guests were below deck at the time, while many of the men had come up to witness the firing. President Tyler was about to join the others but was detained momentarily below deck. A 15-year-old girl who was present later recalled, "Although the president had been summoned twice and his Cabinet awaited him, his voice could still be heard

★ **Explosion aboard the *Princeton* in 1844.**

through the skylight, laughing and talking with Secretary [William] Wilkins over their wine.... The president still lingered in his cabin until a third message reached him, and then he laughingly called out, 'Tell Stockton to go ahead; neither Wilkins nor I like firearms.'"

The gunner reported that the cannon was ready to fire. Then, he recalled, "Captain Stockton came forward, taking his usual position nearest the gun, and in the most exposed place, and, with one foot on the bed, gave his usual order: 'Stand clear of the gun,' and fired her; at which fire the gun burst."

Something had gone horribly wrong. A blinding light lit the sky as the cannon burst into pieces. Sharp fragments of iron flew in every direction, causing damage to the ship and killing Secretary of State Abel Upshur; Secretary of the Navy Thomas Gilmer; David Gardiner, the father of President Tyler's future wife, Julia; and one of the president's servants. Eighteen others were seriously injured.

Foggy Bottom

ALMOST COMPLETELY surrounded by water, the marshy area along the east side of the Potomac known as "Foggy Bottom" was plagued by mosquitoes. By the mid–19th century there were about 600 cases of malaria there per summer, affecting about 20 percent of the area's population. A visiting physician told residents

★ First Presidential Portrait ★

After William Henry Harrison took the oath of office on Inauguration Day, March 4, 1841, he paused to have his photograph taken, becoming the first president to be captured in a photograph while in office. The *daguerreotype* (the earliest form of photography) had just been invented a few years earlier. Unfortunately, nobody knows what became of this image. President Harrison did not survive either, dying just a month after taking office.

★ Ants Infest Georgetown ★

In the summer of 1840, John Laird & Son, tobacco merchants, ordered to Georgetown some vessels to be loaded with tobacco bound for Europe. The ships arrived at the wharves at Frederick Street and the crew tossed out some crates that had been used as ballast. Unfortunately, these crates contained ants that had been taken on board in the West Indies.

Once they arrived in town, the ants multiplied by the thousands. They entered every home and shop as they marched onward due north. They infested the walls of buildings and concealed themselves in all the cracks and openings. These ants could bite, and it sure hurt! They were such a problem that the city offered a reward for their destruction: one dollar per quart for all dead ants brought to the authorities. After paying out several hundred dollars, the city was relieved of this duty when the cold winter of 1840–41 set in and completely destroyed the ants.

of this poor area of the city to cut down vines and shrubs near their homes, put screens in their windows, and light bonfires to keep the mosquitoes away. By his third year there, the number of cases was down to 25 a year.

In the 19th century, Foggy Bottom was home to workers at nearby factories and plants, including the Godey Lime Kilns, the Washington Gas and Light Company, a glass works, and Cranford's Paving Company. One writer described Foggy Bottom in 1893 as "a squalid district whose streets teem with grimy youngsters." Things gradually improved, and now the area contains George Washington University and numerous government buildings, including the Watergate complex, site of the infamous break-in that eventually led to President Richard Nixon's resignation in 1974. Part of Foggy Bottom, with preserved 19th-century homes, is now the Foggy Bottom Historic District.

The *National Era*

WASHINGTON HAS had many newspapers over the years, but the *National Era* was a special kind of newspaper. Established in 1847, it was the city's only antislavery newspaper. It was formed thanks to donations of $20,000 by those opposed to slavery. Dr. Gamaliel Bailey, of Cincinnati, Ohio, was selected as the editor.

Before moving to Washington, Bailey had run an antislavery newspaper called the *Philanthropist* in Cincinnati. In 1836, that newspaper's office was attacked by a mob and the printing press thrown into the Ohio River. The same thing happened again in 1841. In the fall of 1846, Bailey moved to Washington to take the new position, where on January 7, 1847, he produced the newspaper's first issue.

Before it was published as a book, the influential antislavery novel *Uncle Tom's Cabin* first appeared in the *National Era* as a 40-week serial in 1851–1852. Bailey had encouraged author Harriet Beecher Stowe to publish it in the paper.

Revolution in France

THE YEAR 1848 was a monumental one in Europe. Revolution swept through a number of places, including France. Because the French had helped the United States in its Revolutionary War, Americans favored the French citizens in their revolution against the ruling class. The news that King Louis-Philippe had been expelled and a new republic formed brought out celebrations in Washington—a torch-lit procession, bonfires, and a great gathering of people in front of the *Union* newspaper office, where speeches were given to the crowd of

★ *How Dickens Saw It* ★

In 1842, author Charles Dickens described Washington as a city "of spacious avenues that begin in nothing and lead nowhere; streets miles long that want only houses, roads, and inhabitants; public buildings that need but a public to be complete."

cheering onlookers. A senator from Mississippi spoke, saying that "the age of tyrants and slavery was drawing to a close, and that the happy period to be signalized by the universal emancipation of man" was "at this moment visibly commencing."

In the end, despite the optimism, these revolutions did not bring about the change that Europeans and American sympathizers had hoped for.

The *Pearl* Riots

LOCATED AS it was on the border between north and south, Washington had both free and enslaved black residents, and the population was split between people who were pro-slavery and those who opposed it. One free black man, Solomon Northup, who was kidnapped into slavery in Washington in 1853, later told of his experiences in a memoir called *Twelve Years a Slave*, which was made into an award-winning movie in 2013.

Not only was Washington home to thousands of enslaved black residents during the first half of the 19th century, it was also a key slave trading hub. In 1847, a merchant named Daniel Drayton allowed an enslaved woman and her five children and niece on board his ship heading north from Washington, so they could sail to where the woman's husband, a free black man, was waiting. Word of Drayton's good

★ The *National Era* newspaper issue from 1851 that featured the first installment of *Uncle Tom's Cabin*.

deed was spread, and the next year, he was contacted and asked to transport another family up north to freedom. Drayton wanted to help, but now he had no boat. He hired a captain named Edward Sayres, and his ship the *Pearl*, for $100, explaining his mission. Also along was a cook and sailor named Chester English. Drayton bought some timber so he could sell it in Washington and cover the cost of his trip.

On April 13, 1848, the *Pearl*, sailing up the Potomac, anchored on the Maryland side of the river near Point Lookout at Washington. The voyage was supposed to rescue a woman, nine children, and two grandchildren who had

Then and Now Game

TODAY THERE ARE VIRTUALLY no places in Washington that look like they did 200 years ago, but you might be surprised at how many traces of the city at the turn of the 20th century still remain.

In this activity, you'll see for yourself the differences and similarities between the city of the past and the city today.

Adult supervision required

You'll Need
★ Digital camera
★ Computer with word processor
★ Pad of paper and pen
★ Washington, DC, guidebook

On this page are four vintage photographs. Your mission is to head to each of these locations and take a photo from approximately the same vantage point and distance as the old pictures. All four locations are easily accessible via the Metro.

Note some of the interesting-looking buildings and write down their addresses. When you have captured the present-day scenes, upload the images to your computer. Included here are links to the vintage photos on the Library of Congress site. You can download them and lay out each old image next to the new in a word processing document:

www.loc.gov/pictures/resource/npcc
.31234/

www.loc.gov/pictures/resource/ds
.02350/

www.loc.gov/pictures/resource/hhh.dc
0820.photos.042880p/

www.loc.gov/pictures/resource/hec
.31641/

Which buildings in the old photographs are still standing today? How have they changed? What other differences do you notice? (Examples: trees, signs, streets, sidewalks, people, vehicles, etc.) You can use your Washington, DC, guide and the Internet to research the buildings (using the addresses).

Which of the four sites looks the most like it did in the pictures below? Which has changed the most?

★ **The Smithsonian from the Mall, circa 1920.**

★ **Pennsylvania Avenue from the Capitol, 1905.**

★ **Looking northeast on Vermont Avenue, between H and I Streets, circa 1970s.**

★ **Memorial Continental Hall, 17th and D Streets, circa 1922.**

almost succeeded in arguing for their freedom in court but had run out of money and were afraid they would be sold. Upon arriving at the dock, Drayton was told that there were many others who also wanted to escape. Drayton replied that he'd take anyone who was on board the ship by eleven o'clock that night.

As night fell, slaves began to come to the ship. Drayton watched carefully, fearful that they'd be noticed, but they safely set sail with a total of 77 passengers on board, in the hold below the deck. With the lack of wind and the tide against them, they sailed only half a mile before they had to anchor overnight. Drayton went to the hold and distributed bread to the passengers. There were a couple of scares as the little ship sailed 140 miles to the mouth of the Potomac. A steamer from Baltimore and later a schooner passed by, and the passengers seemed to take careful note of what they saw. The winds shifted again and were now against them, and the *Pearl* could not progress any further. They had to take refuge in a place called Cornfield Harbor, near Point Lookout.

Meanwhile, back in Washington, the slaveholders had noticed what had happened, some when they saw there was no breakfast ready for them the next morning. Asking around, they found out that a ship called the *Pearl* had taken the slaves away, and they were eager to

★ **A Washington antislavery flyer from 1836.**

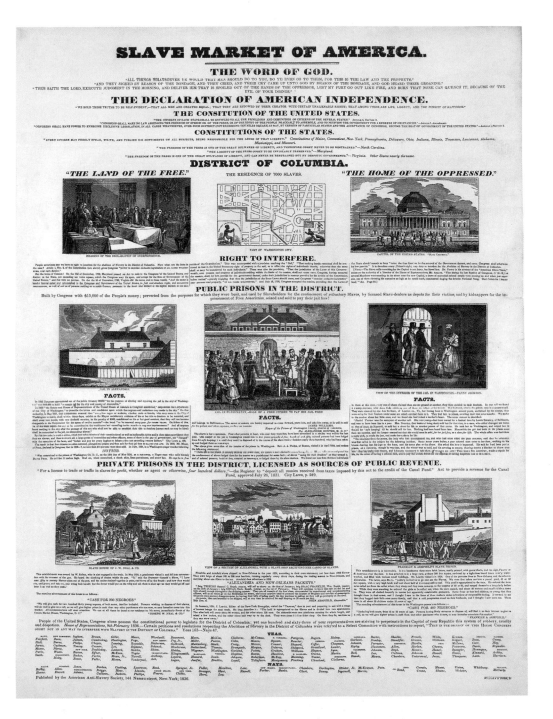

give chase. One of the slaveholders had a small steamboat, and 35 volunteers, including a few slaveholders, set off down the river armed with guns and knives. Passing the steamer from Baltimore and the schooner along the way, they were told that yes, a small sailing ship had passed in the opposite direction. They sailed to the mouth of the Potomac but didn't see the *Pearl*. About to give up the search, they found the *Pearl* at 2 AM, half hidden, anchored at Cornfield Harbor. They pulled up alongside and boarded the *Pearl*, surprising everyone on board. The angry men seized Drayton, Sayres, and English and took them on board the steamboat, leaving the slaves on the *Pearl* and towing it all the way back to Washington.

The boat landed at the steamboat wharf in Washington, a mile from Pennsylvania Avenue. The prisoners and slaves were marched in procession as a growing crowd of onlookers watched. Drayton was almost stabbed by one angry slave trader. As they approached the center of town, the crowd began to chant "Lynch them, lynch them!" For their own protection, Drayton and Sayres were put into a carriage and taken to the jail, with the mob following. The slaves were also put into jail and held as runaways.

The mob next turned its attention to the *National Era* newspaper, which had written about the *Pearl*'s escapades sympathetically. The crowd gathered outside the newspaper office and shouted for Dr. Bailey, the owner/editor of the paper, to come out. He eventually did, saying to them, "I am Dr. Bailey. What is your wish?" They threatened to tar and feather him if he didn't stop publishing his newspaper. He then asked if he could speak in his own defense. The crowd agreed, and he gave an eloquent speech that calmed them. Another Washington citizen, who was known for Southern sympathies, even spoke on Dr. Bailey's behalf

★ **Taken in 1846, this is one of the earliest known photographs of Washington. It shows the General Post Office from the corner of Eighth and E Streets NW, with the shop of Elija Dyer, a tailor, on the left.**

and discouraged violence. The crowd then dispersed without any damage being done.

In the coming days, the slaves were turned back over to the slaveholders, and many of them were sold to slave traders and shipped south. Drayton and Sayres were jailed for four years before receiving a presidential pardon and being set free.

The Smithsonian

WHEN A wealthy Englishman named James Smithson died in Genoa, Italy, in 1829, his will stated, "In case of the death of my said nephew, without leaving a child or children, or in case of the death of the child or children he may have, under the age of twenty-one years, or intestate, I then bequeath the whole of my property... to the United States of America, to found at Washington, under the name of the Smithsonian Institution, an establishment for the increase and diffusion of knowledge among men."

At the time of Smithson's death, his nephew was still alive, but the young man died in 1835, unmarried and without children, at the age of 29. A letter was then sent from London to Washington announcing the gift. Soon afterwards, President Andrew Jackson announced the gift to Congress, where there was some debate as to whether the gift should be accepted. Thanks to a highly favorable report by former president and now congressman John Quincy

Adams, a bill was passed in the summer of 1836 authorizing the president to accept the gift. President Jackson sent a lawyer named Richard Rush to London to pursue the claim in court; two years later the London court accepted and the money was released to Rush. The bequest amounted to 105 bags of money, each containing 1,000 gold pieces—amounting to a total fortune of $508,318.

All this money was waiting to be spent, but it took eight long years to devise a definite plan of action. Some of the nation's respected scholars thought the money should be used to establish a university; others thought a national library. John Quincy Adams favored an astronomical observatory.

In 1840, the National Institution was founded in Washington, to "promote science and the useful arts, and to establish a national museum of natural history." Its membership of 90 prominent Washingtonians often discussed what should be done with the Smithson fund. The idea that the National Institution should be combined with the Smithsonian, bringing all the collections of artifacts owned by the United States together in one building, was rejected.

Finally, after continued debate and inaction from Congress, in 1846 President James Polk signed a bill to incorporate the Smithsonian Institution. The act stated that the institution would house "all of [the] objects of natural history, plants, and geological and mineralogical

★ TOP: **Drawing of the Smithsonian, 1848.**

★ BOTTOM: **Smithsonian "Castle"
as it appears today.**

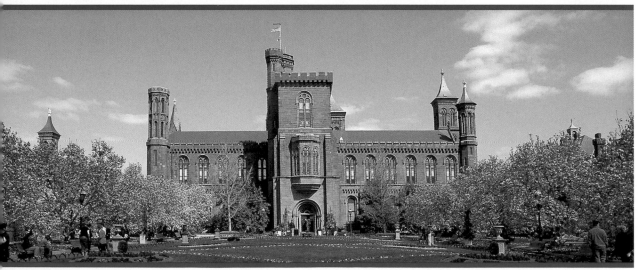

specimens belonging or hereafter to belong to the United States." This included what was known as the "National Cabinet of Curiosities," which was the name for the collection of miscellaneous objects of all kinds.

Joel Poinsett, who had been president of the National Institution, helped mold the Smithsonian into a national museum. The design selected was by James Renwick, a well-known New York architect. Work on the Smithsonian's first building (now known as "the Castle") was begun in 1847 and finished in 1855.

White marble was originally suggested for the Smithsonian, but cheaper and locally quarried red-brown sandstone was chosen instead, giving the building its distinctive look. It was thought to be the first Byzantine-style building in this country that was not a church. It has nine towers of different sizes, the tallest one reaching a height of 145 feet.

The Great Hall of the Smithsonian Institution building was opened to the public in 1855. Prior to that time, the items collected by the Smithsonian were strictly for research purposes and not for public display. In 1858 the Smithsonian acquired specimens from the United States Exploring Expedition, a four-year mission to study the natural world. That began the Smithsonian's journey as a depository for all kinds of specimens of plants, animals, and minerals from around the world. The Smithsonian exhibited at the 1876 Centennial Exposition in Philadelphia, and received enough donations from the exhibitors that the items filled 42 boxcars.

By 1881, there were 250,000 annual visitors to the Smithsonian, and in 1894 the museum's collections numbered a total of 3,279,531 specimens.

At the present day, the Smithsonian consists of 16 different museums, mainly clustered near the original 1855 building. There are currently more than 32 million items in the collection. These days, the phrase "that belongs in the Smithsonian" is commonly used to describe something very old or historically significant.

A Diamond No More

MANY OF the citizens of Alexandria, Virginia, were not thrilled that their city had become part of the District of Columbia. Their first concern was that they were not represented in Congress. And second, they felt ignored by the federal government, whose attentions were focused on improving the city of Washington itself and the parts of the District of Columbia next to it on the Maryland side of the Potomac.

Alexandrians tried as early as 1826 to have their city withdrawn from the District of Columbia. Their first attempt was unsuccessful, but they didn't give up. Between 1830 and 1846, they kept trying to get Congress to take up their cause. The Senate finally agreed to take up the proposal on June 30, 1846. There was some debate between those in favor and those opposed. Senator William Henry Haywood of North Carolina argued that the District of Columbia had been set up by an act of Congress, and just because some of its citizens wanted

out was not reason enough to alter the original intention of the government. Senator John C. Calhoun of South Carolina said there was no reason why it shouldn't happen.

A week later, Congress passed a resolution to allow the territory south and west of the Potomac to be returned to Virginia, providing the citizens voted in favor of it. The vote took place September 1–2, 1846, in the city of Alexandria, and was 763 for, and 222 against. President James Polk officially approved the transfer back to Virginia on September 7, and the District of Columbia was no longer diamond-shaped.

The Washington Monument

In 1783, the Continental Congress adopted a resolution to erect a statue "in honor of George Washington, the illustrious Commander-in-Chief of the United States Army during the war which vindicated and secured their liberty, sovereignty, and independence." However, Washington did not want a statue of himself to be erected while he was still alive, so nothing further was done.

The death of George Washington in December 1799 sent the nation into mourning at the loss of its first president and most esteemed war hero. It wasn't long before the idea of a permanent memorial to the legendary figure was proposed. Just after Washington's death, a resolution was passed by the House of Representatives that "a marble monument be erected by the United States at the Capitol in the city of Washington, and that the family of General Washington be requested to permit his body to be deposited under it; and that the monument be so designed as to commemorate the great events of his military and political life."

Washington's will called for burial at his Mount Vernon estate, not in the city of Washington. His widow, Martha Washington, was also opposed to the Capitol burial idea, but she wrote to President Adams, "Taught, by that great example which I have so long had before me, never to oppose my private wishes to the public will, I must consent to the request made by Congress . . . and, in doing this, I need not, I cannot, say what a sacrifice of individual feeling I make to a sense of public duty."

Despite her consent, the issue became stalled in Congress, and nothing was done for years. The idea of burying Washington at the Capitol came up again in 1829, when architects began to plan a crypt there. Since Martha Washington was now dead, Washington's family was contacted again, and this time the answer was a resounding "No!"

So now, instead of a crypt at the Capitol, a monument within the city was proposed. People around the country began to donate money toward the construction of such a monument. In 1833, the Washington National Monument Society was organized. By the late 1830s, it had raised about $40,000.

On January 26, 1848, a joint resolution granting the site for the monument was passed by the House of Representatives, and approved by the president. The Society originally wanted to build a 600-foot-high flat-topped monument, but later scaled it back to 500 feet with a pyramidal top. Excavation for the foundations was finished by June 1, 1848.

The cornerstone arrived at the Washington rail depot from a quarry in Maryland on June 5. It was brought to the monument site the following day, accompanied by a procession of citizens and a huge American bald eagle sitting atop the stone. This block of white marble weighed 24,500 pounds and measured six feet eight inches square and almost three feet high. The cornerstone was laid in a ceremony on July 4, 1848, attended by 20,000 people, including President Polk, members of his cabinet, and members of Congress. Grandmaster Benjamin French of the Grand Lodge of Free and Accepted Masons of the District of Columbia formally laid the stone, wearing the Masonic apron and sash that had once belonged to George Washington and using the same Mason's gavel Washington had used when he laid the cornerstone of the Capitol Building in 1793. During the ceremony, several mementoes were put into a zinc case within the cornerstone, including copies of the Declaration of Independence and the Constitution and a portrait of George Washington.

In May 1849 some citizens of Alabama proposed to the Monument Society that they donate a custom inscribed block of marble to be placed in the monument. After receiving this offer, the society announced that if any state or any public institution wanted to donate a commemorative stone to be placed in the monument, it would be accepted (along with any accompanying monetary contributions), at a size of four feet long, two feet high, and one foot six inches deep. By the end of June, Georgia, South Carolina, North Carolina, Virginia,

and Delaware proclaimed their intention to donate blocks.

The first memorial stone to be inserted (in October) was from the Franklin Fire Company of Washington, DC, inscribed with the name of the company and "Initiated, 1827. We Strive to Save." The second stone inserted was donated by the secretary of the Washington National Monument Society. By then, the structure had risen 44 feet above the ground. In all, 193 memorial stones were set into the monument.

Money was also donated by individuals and groups, including 40 children from the Washington City Orphan Asylum, who in November 1849 marched to the monument and handed over a donation of one cent each. The citizens of the town of Wheatland, New York, contributed amounts ranging from 50 cents to 50 dollars, totaling more than $1,200. The city of Washington, DC, gave $2,500 to the construction efforts.

Stonemasons earned $1.75 a day, and other workers received $1.00 a day for their efforts. By March 1, 1852, about $130,000 had been raised, and the monument was over one hundred feet high. In the fall of 1852, special collections were taken during the presidential election. In the days and weeks after November 2, donations began to come in, the first being $177.76 from

★ **Proposed design for a monument to George Washington, 1846.**

Cincinnati, Ohio. About $20,000 was raised through the 1852 election campaign.

In 1856, the monument was 174 feet high and had cost $230,000, all that had been raised. Fundraising was very minimal in the years that followed: donations from Mississippi totaled 15 cents, and 48 cents came from Virginia. The Know-Nothing Party (see page 59), which had taken power in the capital, took control of the Washington National Monument Society in the mid-1850s, but almost nothing was accomplished during this period. In fact, legend has it that this anti-Catholic group stole a stone donated by the pope and threw it into the Potomac River!

Finally, in 1876, Congress took over the project and appropriated money—$1 million—to complete it. The design was slightly altered and the foundations were strengthened to support what would be an 81,000-ton structure. The entire cost for the monument was $1,230,000.

By August 1884 the monument was 500 feet high. An additional 55 feet were added for the pyramidal top. The capstone was placed in position December 6, 1884. The Washington Monument was formally opened to the public in 1888. When finished, it was the tallest man-made structure in the world, until the Eiffel Tower was completed in 1889.

★ **Capping the Washington Monument, 1884.**

To Consolidate or Not?

GEORGETOWN PLAYED an important role in the early history of Washington, DC, even though it was not a part of the capital city. For years, it was the older, established nearby town while Washington was still raw and wild. Some were quite happy with Georgetown being a separate city, while others thought it should merge with Washington.

In 1856, a committee from Georgetown met a committee from Washington to come up with a plan for consolidating the two cities into one—Washington. Georgetown would give up its separate existence, become two wards of Washington City, and be represented in the city council. Under this scheme, the cities' debts would be merged, with the citizens sharing in the combined debt of both cities.

Nothing further came of this proposal for some years, and Georgetown remained an independent city until 1870 (see page 78).

The Know-Nothings

DURING THE early 1850s, a new political party sprang up—the Native American Party (later, the American Party), more commonly known as the Know-Nothing Party after the response members were supposed to give when questioned about party activities: "I know nothing." This party was strongly anti-Catholic and

★ John Brown's Raid ★

When abolitionist John Brown seized the federal armory at Harpers Ferry, West Virginia, in October 1859, a force of 106 marines led by Robert E. Lee was sent from Washington to quell Brown's antislavery uprising. The capital, located just 64 miles southeast of Harpers Ferry, was the nearest location of federal forces. Arms were procured by the mayor of the city from the War Department and placed at police headquarters, while special men were mounted and stationed at every highway leading into the city.

anti-immigrant. The year 1854 saw the peak of Know-Nothing power across America. In the fall elections, Know-Nothing candidates won 52 seats in the House of Representatives.

In Washington, the Know-Nothings put forward a city official named John Towers as their candidate for mayor. He won the election. In 1856, Towers declined to run again, and the Know-Nothings put forth Silas Hill as their candidate. The other political parties in Washington were united in their opposition to the Know-Nothings and wanted to defeat them at all cost. They joined forces—Democrats, Republicans, and Whigs—and nominated a doctor and city council member named William Magruder for mayor. It was a tight and vicious race. Magruder won the election by a mere 13 votes out of a total of 5,841!

That was not the end for the Know-Nothings in Washington. Come election time in 1857, the Know-Nothings sent a group of

Make a Cornerstone Box

WHEN THE CORNERSTONE was laid for the addition to the Capitol Building in 1851, Senator Daniel Webster spoke for two hours, telling the audience that he had placed a special note inside the cornerstone that read, "If it shall be the will of God that this structure shall fall from its base, that its foundation be upturned.... Be it known that on this day the Union of the United States of America stands firm, that their Constitution still exists unimpaired, and with all its original usefulness and glory; growing every day stronger and stronger in the affections of the great body of the American people, and attracting more and more the admiration of the world."

The cornerstone for the Washington Monument (1848) contains, among other things, a portrait of Washington, copies of the Constitution and Declaration of Independence, portraits of all presidents and their inaugural addresses, a silver medal of Washington, a Holy Bible, an American flag made of silk, the Washington family coat of arms, and newspapers from several states containing accounts of Washington's death and funeral.

Inside the cornerstone of the Supreme Court Building (1932) is a copy of the 1932 *World Almanac* and a photograph of former chief justice William Howard Taft. The cornerstone of the Jefferson Memorial (1939) contains a copy of the Declaration of Independence and Constitution, several books written by Thomas Jefferson, President Franklin D. Roosevelt's autograph, and copies of the four different Washington newspapers of the time.

In this activity, you will create your own cornerstone time capsule.

You'll Need

★ Variety of small everyday items

★ Box (cardboard, wood, or metal), at least 6 inches by 12 inches and 2 inches deep, with a cover

Imagine that you are in charge of filling a small box to be placed in the cornerstone of a new government building in Washington. What items would you put in it? How would that differ from what you'd put into a box to be buried in your own yard or local park?

Choose a variety of everyday items that represent various aspects of life and of the country today. You could enclose newspaper or magazine articles, photos you've taken, coins or paper money, and a letter you write to someone in the future.

If you're doing this with friends or classmates, exchange boxes when you're done. Whose box do you think gives the most complete and interesting picture of modern life in America?

14 members of a Baltimore street gang called the Plug Uglies to Washington to help turn the election in their favor. The Plug Uglies gathered some additional forces once they arrived in Washington, and headed to the polling place on the south side of Mount Vernon Square between Seventh and Eighth Streets. There, they confronted voters who had been born in other countries, threatening them with knives, clubs, guns, and rocks, and assaulting and driving them away before they had a chance to vote. The crowd eventually grew to more than 500. The scene was a chaotic embarrassment, and the police were unable to stop it. The mayor felt powerless. Desperate, he called on the president to put an end to the chaos.

President James Buchanan ordered United States marines from their Navy Yard barracks to go to the scene. When the force of 110 marines arrived, they were met with jeers and threats by the crowd. The rioters had stolen a brass swivel cannon from a local firehouse, and they threatened to use the cannon on the marines unless they left. General Archibald Henderson gave the order to move in toward the cannon, and led the charge. When he got there, Henderson placed his body against the muzzle to prevent it from being fired at the marines. He said, "Men, you had best think twice before you fire this piece at the marines."

The rioters were not afraid, thinking the marines wouldn't dare fire on them. The general ordered 10 of his men to come retrieve the cannon. The unruly crowd shouted and threw stones at the soldiers, but the marines captured the cannon. General Henderson ordered the men not to fire until they were told. Then, someone in the crowd fired a pistol and the bullet hit one of the marines in the cheek. That was the last straw. The marines opened fire on the crowd. Another bullet from the rioters struck a marine, this time in the shoulder. The marines raised their weapons, preparing to fire off another round. At this point, the crowd finally scattered and the riot was over.

Ten people had been killed in the riot, and 21 were injured. Some of the rioters were arrested and charged with attempting to kill marines. Thankfully, this was the last gasp for the Know-Nothings; they lost power and within a couple of years were finished.

Civil War Days

1860–1880

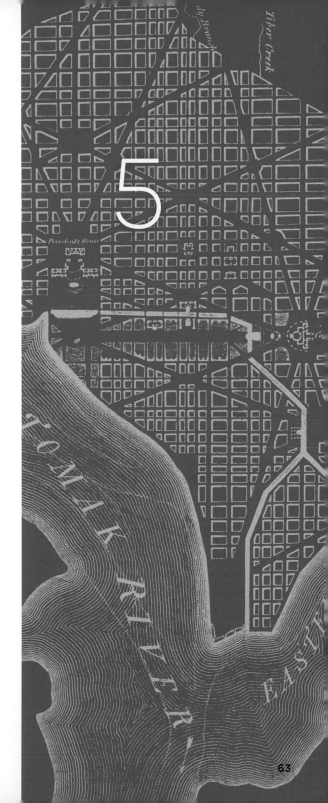

Precariously situated on the border between North and South, Washington was deeply affected by the Civil War. The Confederacy—the 11 Southern states that wanted to leave the Union—was just across the Potomac. Protecting the nation's capital was crucial, and Washington became the place for Union troops to amass. From 1861 to 1865, the city was transformed into an encampment for hundreds of thousands of soldiers, as well as a center for receiving the wounded.

Election Riot

When Abraham Lincoln was elected as the nation's 16th president on November 6, 1860, a riot ensued. Around midnight, a group of about 50 men who supported Lincoln's Democratic opponent, John Breckinridge, were at the Democratic headquarters on Pennsylvania Avenue between Four and a Half and Sixth Streets. The men decided to head to the Republican headquarters at the corner of Indiana Avenue and Second Street with the intention of destroying it. More Breckinridge supporters joined them at Brown's Hotel, and a total of about 300 men headed off toward the Republican headquarters. When they got there, they fired pistols, threw rocks at the windows, broke down the door, and ransacked the place. Finally the police arrived to restore order.

A New Dome

By the 1850s, the old wooden Capitol dome seemed outdated. Not only was it a fire hazard, it also needed frequent repairs. A new dome was desired, one that would create a more impressive look for this building, which by now had been extended to handle a growing number of congressmen as more states were admitted into the Union.

In 1854, the new Capitol architect, Thomas U. Walter, drew a sketch of the building with a bigger, taller cast-iron dome replacing the old wooden dome. He hung this sketch in his office, and members of Congress who saw the drawing were impressed. Before long, his idea was approved in Congress, and in March 1855 President Franklin Pierce authorized $100,000 for the construction of the new dome. The old one was demolished in 1856 and construction began on the new one.

The new dome was to be 142 feet higher than the old one, and much heavier. In order to support the new dome's weight, the Capitol had to be strengthened. The dome and its 8,909,200 pounds of iron would rest on 5,214,000 pounds of masonry. Atop the dome would be a statue of the Goddess of Liberty, capped with eagle feathers. Her right hand would hold a sheathed sword, her left a wreath and shield, and around her forehead would be a ribbon studded with thirteen stars.

The Civil War interrupted the construction, but the exterior of the new dome was completed in December 1863, and the interior work was finished in January 1866. The dome was restored in 1959–1960, but by 2014 it had developed more than 100 cracks and other defects due to age and weather. Starting in 2014, the Capitol began a major $60 million restoration, its first in more than 50 years.

The Civil War

By the time president-elect Lincoln arrived in Washington on February 23, 1861, the country was already splitting in two. John Brown's raid on Harpers Ferry had taken place less than two years earlier, and in the past few months South Carolina had seceded from the Union, followed by Mississippi, Alabama, Florida, and Georgia. Forts in several Southern states had been seized. Several Southern senators had resigned their seats in Congress. Lincoln had arrived secretly, for fear of being assassinated on the way.

March 4 came, and Lincoln was inaugurated. He spoke to the masses gathered before the Capitol Building, concluding his remarks with these words: "We are not enemies, but friends. We must not be enemies. Though passion may have strained, it must not break, our bonds of affection. The mystic cords of memory, stretching from every battlefield and patriot grave to every living heart and hearthstone all over this broad land, will yet swell the chorus of the Union, when again touched, as surely they will be, by the better angels of our nature."

By April, the entire city was abuzz with uncertainty. What would happen if Maryland decided to side with the South? Would Washington remain the capital of the Union, or would it become part of the South? Some

★ **The Capitol dome under construction as seen in March 1861 during Lincoln's inauguration.**

residents sided with the South, some with the North. Nobody knew what would happen next.

The District's militia was called to protect the capital. Within a day, 10 companies were on active duty. Guards were posted at public buildings and at bridges, roads, and the railroad depot. One reporter wrote on April 10, "The city has been the scene of the wildest excitement throughout the day. Troops marching, drums beating, flags flying, the whole length of Pennsylvania Avenue. Ten companies, or one fourth of the volunteer militia of the District are mustering to-day for inspection. Fear of an attack from an invading army . . . is the cause of these movements."

On Thursday, April 11, South Carolina troops opened fire on Fort Sumter. The fort fell on April 13. The citizens of Washington were frenzied. What would this mean for their country? What would it mean for them? People gathered all around the city to speculate and discuss the latest developments.

On the 15th, Lincoln issued a call for 75,000 volunteer troops to defend the Union. Around the country, states responded immediately and telegraphed their pledges of support. New York offered 30,000 men; Vermont sent the message that 1,000 men were ready to march. The governor of Maine said, "The people of Maine of all parties will rally with alacrity to the maintenance of the Government and the Union."

By now, 14 additional companies of District militia had reported, for a total of about 1,400 men in service to protect the city. On April 18 Pennsylvania sent another 500 troops to the capital. The Sixth Massachusetts arrived on the evening of the 19th, battered from encounters with rioters in Baltimore.

The first of the arriving troops went straight to the Capitol. It was quite a scene inside the Senate wing, as the Massachusetts men, exhausted from four days of marching, lay in chairs, on the carpet, or on the tiled Senate floor, using their knapsacks as pillows.

There were now about 3,400 troops in the city, but no more could come for several days. The riots in Baltimore had led to rail service being temporarily stopped from the north. Even as the early troops amassed in Washington, a plot was being discussed by some Virginians to seize control of Washington. The *Richmond Examiner* wrote on April 23, "The capture of Washington City is perfectly within the power of Virginia and Maryland. . . . From the mountain-tops and valleys to the shores of the sea, there is one wild shout of fierce resolve to capture Washington City, at all and every human hazard." Food prices went up because it was harder to get shipments into the city. Hundreds of citizens left Washington because they felt it wasn't safe to remain.

New York's 7th Regiment arrived on April 25, marching down Pennsylvania Avenue, its band playing splendid tunes. More troops from around the Union continued to pour into the capital, both to assure its safety and to prepare for battle wherever one might arise. By April 30, there were 7,500 troops in the city, quartered in the Capitol Building, in the Treasury and Patent offices, at the Navy Yard, and in city hall.

By early summer of 1861, there were more than 50,000 troops stationed in the District of Columbia to protect the capital. Beginning in late May, six forts were quickly built on the Virginia side of the Potomac: Forts Corcoran, Bennett, and Haggerty on the heights over-looking Georgetown, with 23 guns, Fort Runyon with 23 guns, Fort Albany with 18 guns, and Fort Ellsworth on Shuter's Hill overlooking Alexandria with 24 guns. There were no forts on the Maryland side yet.

The troops stayed put for a few months, and then, on July 17, 1861, 30,000 of them began their march south, to engage the Confederate forces at a small stream named Bull Run, near Manassas in northern Virginia. It was quite a spectacle in Washington as the men marched toward battle with bright flags, triumphant music, and a crowd of onlookers. Naturally, the city was anxious to hear news from the battle-front. On the night of July 21, a breathless war correspondent who'd just come from the front told of promising advances by the Union Army. But not long after, this news was updated with the unfortunate: Union retreat and defeat.

Though many Confederate sympathizers had fled the capital by this point, there was still fear of threats from within. In August 1861, government employees in Washington were made to take an oath of allegiance to the Constitution and the Union. More than 100 government workers refused to take the oath and had to abandon their jobs. Even the mayor at first refused to take the oath. He was sent to jail, but after three weeks he changed his mind and pledged his allegiance.

★ **Union troops conducting drills near the Capitol in 1861.**

Things changed quickly in Washington. By October 15, 1861, there were more than 152,000 men encamped in or near the city. By March 1862 the capital was ringed with 151 forts and batteries holding 1,288 guns and mortars—72 south of the Potomac and 79 north of the Potomac. These forts were built of dirt, with walls that were 20 to 25 feet thick at the base, and 12 to 18 feet thick at the parapets. By October 1862 there were 200,000 men camped in a sea of white tents all around the city. Washington was now the most fortified city in the world.

Hospital City

BY THE end of 1862 there were dozens of general hospitals in the city, treating 30,000 sick and injured soldiers. With lots of action taking place in Maryland and Virginia, Washington was the nearest large Union city to many battlefields, and the injured came in by the hundreds every week—by rail, by wagon, and by boat. Many of the hospitals were converted schools, churches, hotels, and even homes. There was a shortage of doctors to treat the injured, and

★ **The 7th New York Cavalry at a camp near Washington City.**

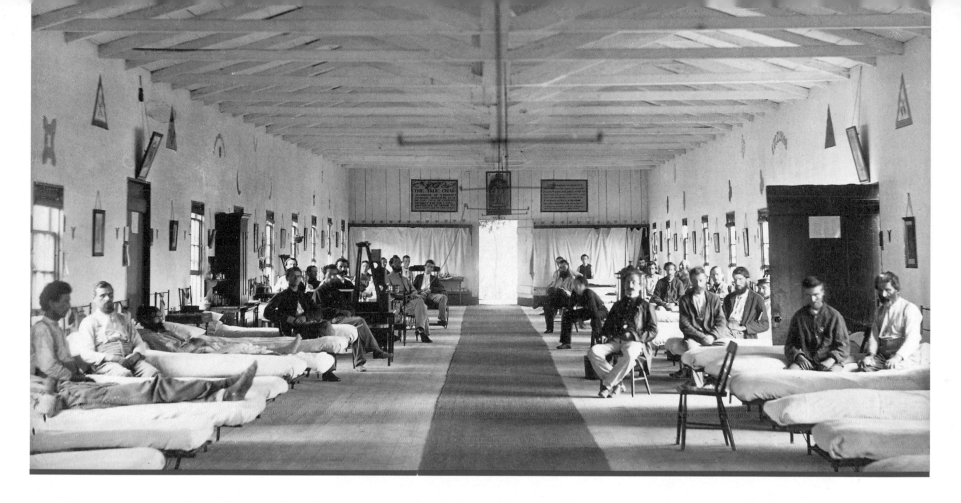

conditions were not good. Bullet wounds and shrapnel injuries often led to infections such as gangrene. For most patients, painkillers were the best they could hope for. Disease and infection killed thousands.

One of the largest and most modern hospitals in Washington was the Armory Square Hospital, composed of 50 wooden buildings, on the Mall near the Smithsonian. Perhaps even more important than the doctors, who could do little, were the nurses, who attended to the patients, played games with them, read to them, and talked to them to help ease their suffering.

One nurse, Amanda Akin, kept a diary during her time at Armory Square Hospital. She recorded her first day working at the hospital: "I meekly followed [the nurse] through the long ward, unable to return the gaze of the occupants of the twenty-six beds, . . . and with a sinking heart watched her raise the head of a poor fellow in the last stages of typhoid, to give

★ **Ward K of the Armory Square Hospital during the Civil War.**

him a soothing draught. Could I ever do that? For once my courage failed."

Even after being there for a while, Amanda said the situation seemed surreal and hopeless. She wrote, "It seemed to me this evening, as I sat at my table adding to the list of medicines—writing down name, regiment, list of clothing, etc., of the new arrivals, calmly looking at the poor maimed sufferers carried by, some without limbs, on a 'stretcher'—that I had forgotten how to feel, it seemed as if I were entirely separated from the world I had left behind."

★ **Walt Whitman in Washington in 1863.**

★ *Keeping in Touch* ★

With hundreds of thousands of men far away from home, camped out in and around the nation's capital, letters flew back and forth in record numbers. Parents, children, siblings, and friends grabbed pen and paper and scrawled notes to their loved ones. Below is an excerpt from a letter written to Fred Silliman, Company H of the 44th Regiment, New York (stationed at Hall's Hill in Arlington, Virginia), by his brother Albert in West Yorkshire, New York, December 1861:

I was glad to hear of your good health and hope it may continue to be so as long as you stay away from home.... We had a grand sight here to the school house Saturday evening, something that never in that place before, a war meeting the house was crowded and crammed.... I asked Eliza if she kissed Bell for you, she says yes 40 times. Mother says she is going to send a blanket, 2 pair of socks, a pair of mittens to you.

The poet Walt Whitman was very active in visiting hospitals and talking to injured soldiers. He favored the Armory Square Hospital in particular. He wrote in a letter to his mother, "I devote myself much to Armory-square hospital because it contains by far the worst cases, most repulsive wounds, has the most suffering and most need of consolation. I go every day without fail, and often at night—sometimes stay very late. No one interferes with me, guards, nurses, doctors, nor any one. I am let to take my own course." Besides keeping patients company, he helped get them medical attention. When he came across Livingston Brooks, a soldier from Pennsylvania who had typhoid and looked to be dying "from negligence and a horrible journey of about forty miles, bad roads, and fast driving" and was now being ignored in the hospital, "I called the doctor's attention to him, shook up the nurses, had him bathed in spirits, gave him lumps of ice, and ice to his head; he had a fearful bursting pain in his head, and his body was like fire."

Emancipation

ON APRIL 16, 1862, Congress passed an act that liberated all enslaved people in the District of Columbia. But this act also compensated slaveholders for their losses. Three commissioners were appointed to pay the

Write a Civil War Letter

DUE TO THE CLOSE PROXIMITY of the Confederacy, Washington, DC, was in quite a precarious location. The defense of the nation's capital was of critical importance during the Civil War. Many key battles were fought in the surrounding areas of Virginia and Maryland. Lots of troops, both Northern and Southern, were stationed near Washington.

In this activity, you'll imagine you are a soldier camped out near the city for the last few weeks and write a letter home. The excerpt below is from an actual letter sent by a soldier from DC back home to Maine in 1864.

While sitting on the east bank of the Potomac last night and hearing the sound of the drum and the roar of the cannon, I thought of home.... We are quartered in a beautiful place and can see miles along the Potomac. We can see Georgetown & Georgetown Heights, also Arlington & Arlington Heights & Fort Jackson & Alexandria all on the west bank of the Potomac, & we can see thousands of tents scattered all along on the heights as far as the eye can read & at sunset it is among the beautifulest scenes I ever saw in my life, & then the Capital & the city is in view in the distance & Fort Washington in the opposite direction which makes a very fine view. We are getting along well now although we had a hard time coming on here and a few days after we camp here but since we came into quarters we get along better, we have plenty to eat now and that is something we didn't get when we first came here, we drill between three and four hours and work as many more so I don't have much time to write and I hasten take my paper on my knapsack or my knee.

Everett M. Arey, December 1864, Washington DC

You'll Need

★ Loose-leaf paper trimmed to 7½ by 9½ inches

★ Pen

★ Half-filled backpack

To properly accomplish this activity, you should try to mimic the conditions under which Everett Arey probably wrote his letter. Go outside with the backpack, pen, and paper at dusk (the most likely time he would have written the above) and sit cross-legged while leaning on your backpack (or your knee) in the fading light and write a letter to your family back home. To make your letter more realistic, you can research battles that took place near Washington, and imagine you are taking part in one of them, or are en route to fight.

Remember to update your family on how you're doing, and also ask how they are doing and for them to write back to you. With the slow mails during the war, your letter (and their reply) might take a while to arrive at its destination. Not only that, paper is scarce too, so use your one sheet well and make each word count. When you are done, fold the paper in eighths so it is about 2½ inches by 4½ inches.

★ The December 1864 letter from Everett Arey to his relatives at home was found tucked in an envelope addressed to him in Washington, postmarked February 1865. Author's collection

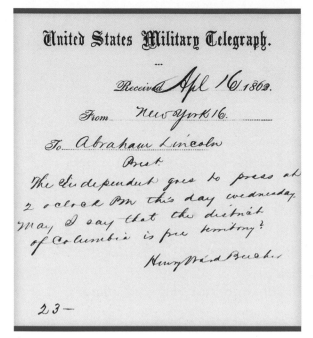

★ **Telegram from Henry Ward Beecher to Abraham Lincoln inquiring whether Washington was now "free territory."**

slaveholders, and the individuals being freed had to undergo an examination by a slave dealer from Baltimore, who'd been hired to help determine what they were worth to their former owners. In city hall, the slave dealer looked at their teeth and made them dance around to see how limber they were. Each person was assigned a value ranging from $10.95 for an infant up to $788.

It took months before the process was completed. A total of $914,942 was paid for the freed slaves and for the expenses of the commissioners. But in the end, 2,989 people were freed.

In September 1862 came President Lincoln's Emancipation Proclamation, which stated that all slaves in the rebelling states were to be freed as of January 1, 1863—with no compensation required to slaveholders.

The Battle of Fort Stevens

THROUGHOUT THE war, there was always a fear that Washington would be attacked and overtaken by the Confederate Army. They were so near, after all. It almost came to pass in July 1864, when General Robert E. Lee ordered General Jubal Early to attack. Early crossed the upper Potomac from Virginia into Maryland with 12,000 troops, and headed toward the capital. Confederate spies had reported that the capital's defense was weakened, and it was

true—there were only 9,000 troops defending the city at that time.

By July 9, Washington residents were frightened, as they could hear the boom of big guns—still miles away in Frederick City, Maryland, but close enough to be heard. Early's troops defeated the Union forces at Frederick, and then marched to Rockville, only about 15 miles from Washington, and camped there on the night of the 10th. The city was in a panic. There were wild rumors about the strength of the Confederate attackers—was it 30,000? 45,000? Government clerks, Navy Yard employees, wagon drivers, and partly disabled war veterans were all armed and sent off to the front or to protect other access points to the city. All the main roads leading into the city were barricaded. General Ulysses S. Grant sent two divisions of the Sixth Corps to protect Washington.

By the morning of July 11, General Early was heading in the direction of Fort Stevens, which lay between what is now 13th Street NW and Georgia Avenue NW. The fort's guns opened fire on Early's men, holding them off for the moment. The Sixth Corps arrived that afternoon, and the next day, the Union Army battled the Confederates and successfully pushed them back. President Lincoln was on hand to witness the fighting from the fort. By the 13th, the Confederates were gone. Washington had been saved from invasion!

★ **Fort Stevens.**

The War Ends

As 1865 began, there was hope that the end of the war was nearing. The Union Army was making progress and the Confederates were running out of steam. A peace conference was held in February between both sides. It failed, but it was still a sign of progress that they could even sit down together.

The citizens of Washington hoped and prayed that it was true, not only for the war to be over, but for their city to be transformed from an encampment back into the capital city. On April 9, 1865, General Robert E. Lee surrendered to General Ulysses S. Grant at Appomattox Court House, Virginia. Fighting continued in spots for some days afterward, but the war was over. The Union was victorious. On April 11, President Lincoln stood on the balcony of the White House and spoke to a crowd that had assembled there. "We meet this evening," he said, "not in sorrow, but in gladness of heart."

The end of the war was officially and joyously celebrated in Washington on April 13. It was declared a holiday, and workers were given the day off. Bands played music in the streets. The Capitol Building, White House, and many other public buildings were covered in decorations and lit by thousands of lights. The Patent Office alone burned 6,000 candles in its windows.

Lincoln Is Assassinated

WITH THE war finally drawn to a close, President Lincoln wanted to have a little relaxation in the city he'd called home for the last four years. What would be the perfect way to relax and celebrate? What about a play? The president had seen many performances since arriving in Washington in 1861, but this one would be extra special, since the conflict that had enveloped his entire presidency was finally over.

On the morning of April 14, the president's messenger went to Ford's Theatre on 10th Street between E and F Streets and reserved a private box for Lincoln; his wife, Mary Todd; and General Grant and his wife, Julia, for that evening's showing of a play called *Our American Cousin*. General Grant had just accepted the surrender of the Confederate Army, and was in Washington to discuss the situation with the president, and to decide on future operations for the speedy establishment of peace. They could both use the diversion, and *Our American Cousin* seemed like the perfect play.

President Lincoln's mind was set not upon revenge but upon bringing peace back to the country. He'd told his cabinet he had "malice toward none," only "charity for all." That day, General Grant got a telegram that called him away to Philadelphia, so instead of Grant and his wife, the Lincolns were accompanied by Major Henry Rathbone and Miss Clara Harris, who was the daughter of a New York senator.

The presidential party arrived after the play had started, but when they entered, the play stopped and the band started playing "Hail to the Chief." The audience got to its feet and applauded and cheered. The president sat in a rocking chair that had been specially placed in the box for him.

Nobody had any idea of what was to come next. During scene two of the third act of the play, a famous stage actor and Confederate supporter named John Wilkes Booth entered the president's box armed with a pistol and a dagger. Booth shot Lincoln in the back of the head from close range. He yelled, "Revenge for the South." Dropping his gun, he took his dagger in his right hand and put his left hand on the railing, getting ready to jump 12 feet down to the stage. Major Rathbone tried to grab him and was cut by the dagger in the process. As Booth jumped down from the box, one of his spurs caught on the large American flag that had been draped underneath the president's box. He tore a piece of the flag and fell, fracturing his leg. He got up, dragging the flag with him partway across the stage, and held the dagger in the air while yelling *Sic semper tyrannis!*" (Latin for "Thus always to tyrants"). He escaped out a back door leading to an alley and rode off on his waiting horse.

The unconscious president was taken across the street to a boardinghouse, now known as the Petersen House, and laid on a bed there. There was nothing anyone could do for him. About 90 visitors filed through during the night to pay their last respects to the dying Lincoln. He died early the next morning at 7:22 AM. Secretary of War Edwin Stanton raised his hat and said, "Now he belongs to the ages."

The assassination of Lincoln was actually part of a bigger conspiracy. There were at least nine people involved in this plot to create chaos in the North. One of the conspirators, Lewis Powell, barged into the home of Secretary of State William Seward at about the same time Booth was carrying out his attack, found Seward in his bedroom, and stabbed him several times. Seward survived, but was not told about Lincoln's death for fear the news would be dangerous to his health. He knew it anyway, though, when he realized something must be terribly wrong if Lincoln was not the first to visit him in his sickbed. Seward recovered and would go on to gain fame for his purchase of Alaska from Russia in 1867.

Another conspirator, George Atzerodt, had agreed to assassinate Vice President Andrew Johnson, but he lost his nerve and never made the attempt. When Lincoln passed away, Johnson was sworn in as president.

Mourning Loss and Celebrating Peace

PRESIDENT LINCOLN'S body was taken to the White House on April 15, where it remained until it was removed to the rotunda of the Capitol Building on the 19th. The procession was led by 30,000 troops, government officials, and citizens. Lincoln's coffin lay in state in the Capitol, and April 20 was the day for the public to pay their respects to the fallen president. An estimated 40,000 people filed past the coffin. On the morning of April 21, Lincoln's coffin was taken to the Baltimore

★ **Ford's Theatre playbill from April 1865.**

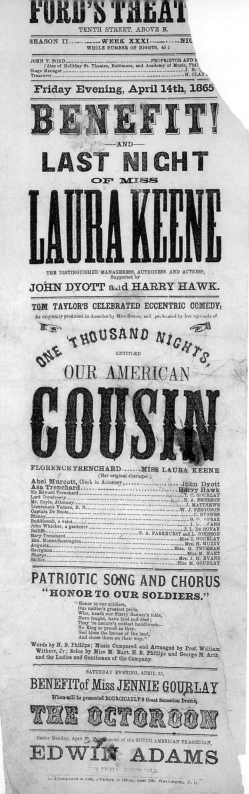

FORD'S THEAT
TENTH STREET, ABOVE E.
SEASON II .... WEEK XXXI .... NIG
WHOLE NUMBER OF NIGHTS, 495

JOHN T. FORD .... PROPRIETOR AND
Stage Manager ....
Treasurer .... H. CLAY

Friday Evening, April 14th, 1865

BENEFIT!
—AND—
LAST NIGHT
OF MISS
LAURA KEENE

THE DISTINGUISHED MANAGERESS, AUTHORESS AND ACTRESS,
Supported by
JOHN DYOTT and HARRY HAWK.

TOM TAYLOR'S CELEBRATED ECCENTRIC COMEDY,
As originally produced in America by Miss Keene, and performed by her upwards of

ONE THOUSAND NIGHTS,
ENTITLED
OUR AMERICAN
COUSIN

FLORENCE TRENCHARD .... MISS LAURA KEENE
(Her original character.)
Abel Murcott, Clerk to Attorney .... John Dyott
Asa Trenchard .... Harry Hawk
Sir Edward Trenchard .... T. C. GOURLAY
Lord Dundreary .... E. A. EMERSON
Mr. Coyle, Attorney .... J. MATTHEWS
Lieutenant Vernon, R. N. .... W. J. FERGUSON
Captain De Boots .... C. BYRNES
Binney .... G. C. SPEAR
Buddicomb, a valet .... J. L. EVANS
John Whicker, a gardener .... J. L. De BONAY
Bailiffs .... G. A. PARKHURST and L. JOHNSON
Mary Trenchard .... MISS J. GOURLAY
Mrs. Mountchessington .... MRS. H. MUZZY
Augusta .... Miss. H. TRUEMAN
Georgiana .... Miss M. HART
Sharpe .... MRS. J. H. EVANS
Skillet .... Miss M. GOURLAY

PATRIOTIC SONG AND CHORUS
"HONOR TO OUR SOLDIERS."

"Honor to our soldiers,
Our nation's greatest pride,
Who, neath our Starry Banner's folds,
Have fought, have bled and died;
They're nature's noblest handiwork—
No King so proud as they,
God bless the heroes of the land,
And cheer them on their way."

Words by H. B. Phillips; Music Composed and Arranged by Prof. William
Withers, Jr.; Solos by Miss M. Hart, H. B. Phillips and George M. Arth
and the Ladies and Gentlemen of the Company.

SATURDAY EVENING, APRIL 15,
BENEFIT of Miss JENNIE GOURLAY
When will be presented BOURCICAULT'S Great Sensation Drama,
THE OCTOROON

Easter Monday, April 17, ... present of the YOUNG AMERICAN TRAGEDIAN,
EDWIN ADAMS

★ *What Became of Ford's Theatre and the Petersen House?* ★

THE HOUSE IN WHICH

ABRAHAM LINCOLN

DIED

516 Tenth Street Northwest

WASHINGTON, D. C.

CONTAINS THE

Oldroyd Lincoln Memorial Collection

CONSISTING OF

OVER THREE THOUSAND ARTICLES
PERTAINING TO THE MARTYRED PRESIDENT

Open Every Day and Evening at all Hours

Ford's Theatre was bought by the government in 1866 for $88,000, and was first used to house the Army Medical Museum and the record and pension division of the Office of the Surgeon General. The interior was entirely reconstructed, leaving no trace of the scene of the assassination. In 1893, part of the building's interior collapsed, killing 22 people. In 1932, the former theater became a Lincoln museum, and finally, in 1965, a restoration was begun to turn it back to its original appearance at the time of the assassination.

The bedroom in the Petersen House where Lincoln died was stripped of its original furniture and in the late 19th century was used as a playroom by the owner's children. Then, from 1896 to 1930, the building was a museum run by Osborn Oldroyd, who had an extensive collection of Lincoln memorabilia. The National Park Service acquired the house in 1933 and turned it into a museum.

★ **Pamphlet for the house where Lincoln died, 1898.**

and Ohio Railroad Station and placed on a train heading to Springfield, Illinois, where he was to be buried. Flags remained at half-mast in Washington for six weeks.

Despite the nation's great loss, the capital continued to pay tribute to the end of the war and the brave soldiers who had made it possible. On May 23 and 24, thousands of Union troops marched through the streets prior to being disbanded. The 23rd was set as the day for the Army of the Potomac, and the 24th for the Division of the Mississippi. There were so many visitors that every available hotel and boardinghouse was filled to capacity. Many visitors had to sleep on park benches or spend the night wandering the streets.

Banners and flags were waved, and thousands of cheering and applauding people turned out to see and thank the soldiers for their efforts, giving garlands to them as they passed. Bayonets gleamed in the sun and bugles blared as more than 200,000 soldiers marched proudly on the first day. There were decorated reviewing stands in front of the White House set up for the president and his cabinet, congressmen, governors, and disabled veterans. President Johnson and General Grant watched in approval as the troops passed. Two thousand schoolchildren along with their teachers were positioned on the north side of the Capitol. The girls were decorated with colored ribbons, and the boys wore colorful rosettes on their chests.

All held flags and banners and sang "Battle Cry of Freedom," in honor of the returned soldiers. One by one the war heroes people had read about in the newspapers—General William Tecumseh Sherman, General George Meade, General George Armstrong Custer, and many others—marched through Washington.

Pretty City

In 1865, journalist and politician Horace Greeley echoed the feelings of many visitors when he complained about conditions in the nation's capital: "The rents are high, the food is bad, the dust is disgusting, the mud is deep, and the morals are deplorable." But as the decades passed, Washington began to look more and more like the majestic city it is today. In February 1871, Washington celebrated the paving of Pennsylvania Avenue, with wood replacing cobblestones. Landscaping of the city finally got serious in 1872, when the District's Department of Public Works created a "Parking Commission" and began to plant shade trees all across the city. (In those days, long before the invention of the automobile, *parking* meant rendering an area more parklike by improving roadsides with soil, grass, and trees.)

At first the trees were purchased from local nurseries but before long the city began to grow its own trees from seed. By 1887 a total of 63,000 shade trees had been planted in Washington, including 27,000 maple, 7,000 poplar, and 10,000 elm and linden trees. The trees provided shade that made the city more tolerable in the summer and helped keep the air fresh year-round.

African American Freedom

The African American population of Washington elected several black representatives to the city council between 1866 and 1871. There were now free schools for blacks, and discrimination was officially frowned upon in the city.

One of the biggest milestones in helping freed slaves fit into society was the establishment of Howard University in 1867. The university is named for General Oliver Otis Howard, who was at the time in charge of the Freedmen's Bureau, responsible for trying to integrate freed slaves into society. He served as the university's president from 1869 to 1872.

Though it was founded to help freed slaves obtain an education and continued to serve African American students, it was not until 1926 that Howard University had its first black president.

Territorial Government

The 1868 mayoral election results were highly disputed, with both Democrats and Republicans declaring their candidate the victor. The

ACTIVITY

Design a Memorial

GEORGE WASHINGTON, Thomas Jefferson, Franklin Roosevelt, and Abraham Lincoln all have memorials in Washington, DC. If you had to pick another former president or other important person (no longer living) to so honor, who would it be? What would you design for them to commemorate their life and contributions to our country, and where would you place it within DC?

Write a one-page speech to propose your idea to Congress—your classmates. Make arguments as to why this person is worthy and explain why you chose your site. Draw sketches of your proposed memorial or monument, to present with your speech. After each person in your class takes a turn, the class should vote yes or no as to whether the idea is a good one. See which idea gets the most votes.

apparent winner, by 83 votes, was the Republican, Sayles Bowen, but it was so close that the vote was recounted by a committee with members from both parties. In the meantime, the city council named a third person, Thomas Lloyd, as acting mayor until the mess could be sorted out. Despite this, Bowen took control of the office and refused to give it up.

As a result of this conflict, in 1870 a group of citizens began a movement for changing Washington's form of government. They felt that the existing system was not working. A committee of 150 people was appointed to look into the matter. Committee members wrote a bill that made its way to Congress, which passed it on February 21, 1871. The elected mayor system of government that had been in place for 50 years was abolished.

The government of Washington, DC, would now be similar to that of a US territory, with a presidentially appointed governor and Legislative Assembly (consisting of 17 members) and House of Delegates (consisting of 46 members) elected by adult male citizens, including one official delegate to Congress. Under this new rule, all territory in the District of Columbia was now part of Washington; Washington City no longer existed as a separate entity. This meant that Georgetown was no longer a separate city but a part of Washington, DC.

Not everyone was pleased with the new form of government, however. Some Washingtonians complained that nothing was getting done, and after an investigation by Congress, the territorial government was abolished in 1874 and replaced by a three-man Board of Commissioners appointed by the president. In 1878, the law was changed again, specifying that two of the president's choices were to be civilians who had lived in DC for at least three years and who had to be confirmed by the Senate, and an officer from the army. The two civilians would receive $5,000 a year, but the army officer would not be paid anything above his regular army salary. The head, or president, of the Board of Commissioners, was the one who officially ran the city and served as its chief executive. This form of government stayed in place until 1967, when the system was changed once again on the path to "home rule" for DC residents (see page 114).

Center Market

A LARGE public market in Washington was originally George Washington's idea, and a few years after his death, a city ordinance in 1802 approved the establishment of the Center Market at Pennsylvania Avenue, between Seventh and Ninth Streets, about halfway between the White House and the Capitol. Washington residents could come here to buy produce and provisions from a variety of vendors.

The original Center Market building was designed by James Hoban, the architect of the

White House. In the early days, it was also called Marsh Market, because of the creek that ran behind it, allowing fish sellers to keep live fish in wire baskets lowered into the water until purchased. Other markets would follow (including Western Market, Eastern Market, and Northern Liberty Market), but the Center Market was the largest. Despite a lot of money spent on improvements over the years—new buildings, paving, leveling of the ground—by the 1850s, Center Market was a disorganized collection of buildings and sheds.

In a 1922 speech, an elderly man named Washington Topham recalled the Center Market of those days: "As a boy I used to go in and out of the old Centre Market, before the present splendid structures were built," he said, "and I well remember their quaint appearance, the old wooden sheds, the low, soiled, white-washed, weather-beaten walls, with the green moss growing over the shingled roof and hanging from the eaves."

Finally, in 1871, a large and impressive market building was constructed. It was one of the largest markets in the country. At its peak there were nearly 700 dealers who rented space in the market, selling a huge range of fruits and vegetables. With improvements in transportation, the markets could now sell produce from around the country and across the world. The market opened early every weekday morning, and that was when the best quality produce

★ The Center Market, seen in the 1920s.

was to be found. It closed by mid-afternoon, except on Saturdays, when it was open all day. The building was demolished in 1931 to make way for the National Archives Building.

The Botanic Garden

THE UNITED States Botanic Garden was founded in 1820 opposite the western side of the Capitol Building, from First Street to Third Street between Pennsylvania and Maryland Avenues. The first greenhouse was built in 1842 to house a collection of exotic plants brought back from an expedition to the South Seas. The Garden was first opened to the public in 1850 and has been open ever since. By the 1870s the Botanic Garden featured an impressive 300-foot-long glass and iron greenhouse building. Some of the plants on display then were exotics that Americans had never seen before, such as a cinnamon tree, banana plant, coffee plant, rubber tree, bread tree, guava tree, and vanilla bush.

The Botanic Garden moved to its present location in 1933, a complex located along Independence Avenue bordered by First and Third Streets. It was run by the Library of Congress starting in 1856, and then by the Architect of the Capitol since 1933. Its centerpiece is the glass greenhouse dating to 1933, and restored in 2001.

Arlington National Cemetery

DURING THE Civil War, it was hard to find burial space for all the war dead. The government started to bury soldiers on property in Arlington, Virginia, that belonged to Confederate General Robert E. Lee, through his wife, a descendant of Martha Washington. The Lee family had left in 1861, and Union troops used the property as a camp. (A couple of years later, the government created a place called Freedman's Village on the

★ **The historic conservatory at the United States Botanic Garden.**

80

property to help slaves make the transition to a life of freedom.) Private William Christman was the first soldier to be buried at the site, on May 13, 1864. By June the War Department had set aside 200 acres of the Lee property for use as a cemetery.

By the end of the Civil War in 1865, thousands of service members and former slaves had been buried at Arlington. The Lees were eventually compensated for the property and the cemetery grew in prominence as the years passed.

Today there are more than 400,000 men and women buried in the cemetery. Among the famous people buried there are Pierre L'Enfant, presidents Taft and Kennedy, 12 Supreme Court justices, explorers Admiral Richard Byrd and Robert Peary, the boxer Joe Louis, civil rights leader Medgar Evers, Edward Kennedy and Robert Kennedy, Jacqueline Onassis (widow of President Kennedy), and the novelist Dashiell Hammett.

The Tomb of the Unknown Soldier in Arlington is one of the nation's best-known memorials. It includes remains of unknown service members from World War I, World War II, and the Korean War, and is guarded 24 hours a day, year-round.

 Arlington National Cemetery in spring.

★ ★ ★

The Making of a Capital City

1880-1930

It took some time, but by the late 19th and early 20th centuries, Washington, DC, was finally becoming the city it was destined to be. At this point, 100 years after its founding, it began to look more like Pierre L'Enfant's original vision. It was becoming the Washington we see today.

Another President Is Shot

EARLY IN the summer of 1881, the year he assumed office, President James A. Garfield decided to take a two-week vacation in New England. He'd be traveling with his family and several cabinet members.

Garfield was to arrive at the Baltimore and Potomac Railroad Station in Washington on July 2, 1881, at 9:30 AM. Others in his party showed up first. The president's carriage was last to arrive at the station, shortly after 9:20 AM. Garfield and his companion, Secretary of State James Blaine, entered the depot through the main entrance on B Street. The pair had only walked 10 feet when two loud cracks were heard. The president fell to the floor, struck by two bullets, one in the shoulder and the other in the back. The shooter was Charles Guiteau, a mentally unstable lawyer who had written a speech in support of Garfield's election and was upset that the president wouldn't give him a government position in Paris in return.

Help was summoned, and a doctor arrived within four minutes. The news spread rapidly, and within 10 minutes a crowd had gathered at the corner of B and Sixth Streets. The doctor ordered that Garfield be carried to a room upstairs, away from the crowds. Another doctor arrived and the president asked how his wounds looked. The doctor said they did not seem serious. The president replied, "I thank you, doctor, but I am a dead man." The doctors decided to take Garfield by ambulance to the White House.

He clung to life in the White House for the rest of July and all of August, and in early September it was decided he should be taken to Long Branch, New Jersey, to get some fresh ocean air. He died there on September 19, and Vice President Chester A. Arthur was sworn in as the new president. Guiteau was tried, found guilty, and executed in 1882 in Washington.

A Gift of Cherry Trees

IN 1885, a writer and photographer named Eliza Ruhamah Scidmore returned to Washington from a visit to Japan with an interesting idea. She proposed to the Washington superintendent of the Office of Public Buildings and Grounds that cherry trees be planted along the waterfront of the Potomac River. She'd seen the beautiful flowering trees in Japan and thought they would look lovely in Washington. Though her idea was not embraced at the time, she didn't give up. She kept trying to propose the planting of cherry trees to each new superintendent over the next 24 years.

Meanwhile, in 1906, a government official named Dr. David Fairchild imported 100 cherry trees from Japan and planted them on his own property in Maryland to see how they would do. The trees did well and Dr. Fairchild was pleased. He donated cherry trees to the children of the various schools in DC.

In April 1909 Mrs. Scidmore wrote to the new First Lady, Helen Herron Taft, with the idea of raising money to purchase cherry trees and then donate them to the city. Mrs. Taft replied:

Thank you very much for your suggestion about the cherry trees. I have taken the matter up and am promised the trees, but I thought perhaps it would be best to make an avenue of them, extending down to the turn in the road, as the other part is still too rough to do any planting. Of course, they could not reflect in the water, but the effect would be very lovely of the long avenue. Let me know what you think about this.

Sincerely yours,
Helen H. Taft

Shortly after, the Japanese consul heard about the plan to plant cherry trees in DC and liked the idea so much he asked Mrs. Taft whether the city would accept a donation of additional trees from the City of Tokyo. The gift of 2,000 cherry trees from Japan arrived in Seattle, Washington, on December 10, 1910, and traveled almost a month to arrive in DC on January 6. Sadly, on January 19, government inspectors found the trees to be infested with insects. The trees were destroyed.

Though there were fears that this might cause strain in American-Japanese relations, the Japanese were understanding, and a second donation was made, this time of 3,020 trees. They arrived in DC on March 26, 1912. The very next day, Mrs. Taft and the Viscountess Iwa Chinda (the Japanese ambassador's wife) planted two cherry trees on the northern bank

★ RIGHT: **First page of a 1911 letter from the wife of Tokyo's mayor regarding the donation of cherry trees.**

★ BELOW: **Cherry tree in bloom on the Mall in April.** Author's collection

225, SHINAGAWA,
TOKIO.

Feb. 26th 1911

My dear Mrs Taft,

on the 14th of February by the "Awa Maru" via San Fran co my husband shipped off 3000 cherry trees which he hopes will form an avenue in Washington as a

Plant a Cherry Tree

MOST OF THE ORIGINAL cherry trees that were given by Japan to the United States in 1912 are long gone. There are only a handful left; the rest are replacements planted later. All the DC cherry trees are ornamental, meaning they do not bear any edible fruit.

In this activity you can try your hand at growing your own cherry tree—a fruit-bearing variety!

You'll Need
★ 1 dozen fresh cherries
★ Plastic container with a lid
★ Bag of potting soil
★ 2 pots, 6 inches in diameter (for indoor planting in spring or summertime)
★ Plastic spoon
★ Trowel

Cherry pits, which are inside all cherries, can become cherry trees. But you have to take a few steps to make sure they grow. First, eat the cherries and remove the pits. Wash them off, removing any bits of fruit. Then, set the pits out to dry for a few hours.

Place moistened potting soil into a plastic container, and put the cherry pits in amid the soil. Place the container in the refrigerator and leave in there for about 10 to 12 weeks, checking to make sure the soil is still moist every week. After that time has passed, you're ready to plant.

You can plant in a pot indoors in the late spring or summer months or directly outside (2 feet apart) in the late fall or winter, using a plastic spoon (for a pot) or a trowel (for outdoors) to dig the holes. You should plant all the pits, since probably only a few will sprout. It does take weeks for the plants to sprout, so be patient and keep watering! If you've planted in a pot, transplant the seedlings outside when it starts to get cold. Keep the soil moist no matter where you've planted them.

After a year or so, if more than one seedling has sprouted, and you want to have more than one tree (and have space for it), plant them about 25 to 30 feet apart. The tree won't bear fruit for about seven years, but if you're lucky, after that you'll have a cherry tree. You'll notice that your tree will have flowers, though they won't be as vibrant and profuse as the ornamental cherry trees in Washington.

★ Sakiko Saito, the daughter of the Japanese ambassador, is crowned Queen of the Cherry Blossoms in 1937.

of the Tidal Basin. The National Cherry Blossom Festival was born from this first ceremonial planting, and workers continued to plant the rest of the trees over the next few years.

In 1965, the Japanese government donated another 3,800 trees to the city. Many of these were planted on the grounds of the Washington Monument.

The National Zoo

ONE OF Washington's major attractions is the National Zoo, which is part of the Smithsonian. The 163-acre zoo first came into existence in 1887 as an exhibit located on the National Mall behind the original Smithsonian building, showcasing bison and a few other native North American species.

In 1889, Congress passed an act establishing the National Zoological Park, to be dedicated to "the advancement of science and the instruction and recreation of the people." The zoo is now located about 2.5 miles north of the White House. There are over 2,000 animals of 400 different species represented in the zoo.

Union Station

BY THE late 19th century, coal-burning trains running through the center of the city had become a real problem. The Baltimore and Potomac Railroad, for example, had a station

★ **Washington at the turn of the 20th century.**
Author's collection

located where the National Gallery of Art is today. Every day there were more than 205 locomotives in use in Washington, each one pouring smoke into the sky that polluted the air and discolored the buildings.

When the Pennsylvania and the Baltimore and Ohio Railroads announced in 1901 their plans to build a new rail terminal in Washington, people in the city celebrated. The construction of the new Union Station meant that all of DC's rail lines could be consolidated in one building—one big station instead of several. It also meant that the unsightly railroad tracks and terminals on the Mall would finally be removed.

The new Union Station faced the Capitol, which was five blocks to the west. It had an elegant neoclassical facade 600 feet long (the size of two football fields). The ceiling in the waiting room was 96 feet high. Materials used included marble, granite, and gold leaf.

During the 1940s, as many as 200,000 people passed through Union Station every day. Later, with the growing use of automobiles and airplanes, its popularity declined. In the 1960s and '70s, the government decided to turn it into a visitor center. The station was closed for several years and then reopened in 1988 with shops, restaurants, and movie theaters occupying the original building, and a new Amtrak terminal at the back. Today Union Station is again one of Washington's busiest and best-known places, with 20 million visitors each year.

★ **Union Station in 1907, just after its completion.**

The Safety Train

IN THE early 20th century, with millions of people working in dangerous conditions and with dangerous machines on a daily basis, accidental injuries and deaths were common. The federal government decided in February 1916 that it would be useful to put on a display about safety, so the public could learn more about ways they could avoid injury or death or damage to their property.

An exhibit was put together and shown at the Smithsonian for six days. It included a display by the Bureau of Mines about rescuing miners from poisonous gas, one from the Public Health Service about contagious diseases, and exhibits from the US Army and the Department of Agriculture, among others. Twenty-five federal bureaus, the Red Cross, and the Washington police department participated. A total of 35,000 people visited the exhibition, and government officials wished that the exhibit could be shown all across the country.

What if they could create a Government Safety-First Special Train? The president of the Baltimore and Ohio Railroad agreed to loan the government a twelve-car train to carry the exhibits around the country by rail. The displays were quickly set up in the train cars, and the special Safety Train was ready to leave Washington on May 1.

President Woodrow Wilson and many of his cabinet members were present to walk through the train before it departed from Union Station. In nine weeks the train visited 50 towns across the country, receiving 318,000 visitors.

The Making of the Mall

ONE OF Washington, DC's most distinctive features today is the National Mall, a two-mile stretch of open space that runs from the Capitol to the Potomac River. But that wasn't always the case. Though the Mall was part of Pierre L'Enfant's original plan for the city, it was not named that until it appeared on an 1802 map drawn by Mathew Carey.

★ Pie City ★

Pie was a very popular dessert treat in the Washington, DC, of old. In the late 19th century, the National Pie Bakery on East Capitol Street could churn out 3,000 pies a day. Five wagons delivered the pies around the city. The Connecti-cut Pie Bakery on 32nd Street offered many varieties: apple, mince, lemon, peach, grape, cranberry, prune, whortleberry, pineapple, currant, gooseberry, blackberry, raspberry, cherry, strawberry, custard, and coconut.

★ Visiting President Wilson ★

Reverend Francis B. Sayre Jr. (1915–2008) was the dean of the National Cathedral in Washington, DC, for 27 years and was President Woodrow Wilson's grandson. In an interview with the author in 2001, Sayre remembered:

I was born in the White House and am the last one to have been born in the White House. I have a vivid memory [of Woodrow Wilson] because I saw a great deal of him, since we lived not far away, just within walking distance of where he lived. I was his first grandchild, he lived just down the street, a few blocks, in his house which he owned all the time he was in the White House. That's where I got to know him best. He was a busy man, very busy. But he rather enjoyed seeing his first grandchild, and I enjoyed seeing him a great deal. We talked politics.

★ **The National Mall today.**

And for many decades, the only landscaped part of the Mall was the Capitol grounds.

An 1822 plan for the landscaping of the eastern end of the Mall was not implemented. A few decades later, while designing the new Smithsonian building's landscaping, architect Robert Mills designed a landscape plan for the entire Mall, but this was not carried out, either. In 1850, President Millard Fillmore asked a landscape designer to develop a plan for the Mall. The plan was completed in 1851,

but the designer died in 1852, and his plans went nowhere.

By the time the Smithsonian Castle was completed in 1855, the Mall was largely unfinished, not at all the parklike space L'Enfant had imagined. Railroad tracks crossed it, buildings encroached on it, and parts were swampy. Improvements and additions, such as a few gardens here and there, were made very slowly. During the Civil War, troops used the Mall as training grounds; cattle grazed near

Mall Walking Tour

THE NATIONAL MALL receives 25 million visitors a year. This walking tour highlights the history of, and interesting facts about, some of the many attractions along the National Mall.

Begin walking at the grounds just west of the **Capitol Building**, which is the first part of the Mall that was landscaped (for many years it was the only part). The government's first priority was building all the necessary federal buildings, not landscaping. Realizing Pierre L'Enfant's full vision would take many years.

As you walk west toward the **Washington Monument**, you will note the **National Gallery of Art** on your right, and the **National Museum of the American Indian** on your left. The west building of the gallery is the original, completed in 1937 with money from the philanthropist Andrew Mellon, who donated not only money for the building, but also his art collection. Within a few decades, the collections outgrew the museum, and an east building was constructed, completed in 1978. The Museum of the American Indian is a very recent addition to the Mall; it opened in 2004.

On your left at Sixth Street is the **Air and Space Museum**, completed in 1976, which houses the Wright Brothers' Kitty Hawk plane and the *Apollo 11* space capsule.

Where you are standing now, at Sixth Street, is roughly where the Baltimore and Potomac Railroad Station was in the late 1800s. Looking west, imagine what the Mall used to look like during the Civil War, when troops paraded here.

As you pass Seventh Street, you'll see the **Hirschhorn Gallery** (which opened in 1974) on the left and the six-acre **National Sculpture Garden** on the right. By the time you get to Ninth Street, on your left, you'll see the historic **Arts and Industries Building**, opened in 1881. For decades, this building and the **Smithsonian Castle**, up ahead on the left, were the only two museum buildings on the Mall—until the large, green-domed building on the right was completed in 1910, the **National Museum of Natural History**. The museum is the size of 18 football fields and has 1,000 employees.

As you keep walking, you'll get a better view of the Castle, the original Smithsonian building, on your left (see page 54 for more details). Behind it are three more museums—the **Freer Gallery** (completed 1921), the **Sackler Gallery** (completed 1987), and the **National Museum of African Art** (completed 1987).

As you cross 12th Street, you'll see the final museum on the central strip of the Mall, on your right—the **National Museum of American History**, which opened in 1964 and contains more than 3 million artifacts—everything from cash registers to quilts to bathtubs. You'll also see the only building on the Mall that is not a museum: the **Department of Agriculture building**, which was completed in sections, starting in 1908. The Agriculture Department originally intended the building to be in the center of the Mall, but President Theodore Roosevelt's intervention prevented that.

When you reach 14th Street and head to the left (south), you'll pass the **United States Holocaust Memorial Museum**, which opened in 1993.

Design a New Flag for DC

CHARLES A. R. DUNN was a talented magazine illustrator who in 1917 was working as an engraver on a special edition of *National Geographic* featuring flags of the world. As he worked, he noticed that the flag that would represent Washington, DC, seemed unworthy of such an important city. In fact, the District had no official flag, and the magazine was planning to use the flag of the DC Militia instead, which showed a hatchet on a field of blue with the word "Headquarters" above and "District of Columbia Militia" below.

Though he didn't do anything about it immediately, Dunn never forgot this. After serving in World War I, Dunn came up with the idea of using the coat of arms of George Washington's family as the basis for a flag design. It consists of three red stars above two horizontal red stripes on a white field. In 1924, Dunn sent his concept to the *Washington Evening Star*, a local newspaper. It so happened that the very same year, the Senate District Committee took up the topic of deciding on an official flag for the city. Nothing happened for years, but in 1938, Dunn's design was selected from various submissions and became the official flag of the District of Columbia.

If you were to create a new flag for the city of Washington, DC, what would it look like? Using pencil first, sketch a few possible ideas. When you have one you like, plot out what colors you'd like to use and where. Use markers to color in the various parts of your design.

★ The flag of Washington, DC.

the unfinished Washington Monument. In 1882, parts of the Potomac were dredged, and the silt and soil that was recovered was used to extend the Mall to the west.

Finally, in 1902, the McMillan Commission, a panel of two architects, a landscape architect, and a sculptor, reported that the original concept was mostly a good one and should be fully implemented. Eventually the train tracks were removed, trees were planted, and landscaping was done to make the entire Mall pedestrian-friendly. The Mall finally began to take on its current appearance.

The Height of Buildings Act

WHEN THE 164-foot-high, 12-story Cairo Hotel was built on Q Street in 1894, there were complaints that it was a fire hazard and that it blocked light and views in the neighborhood. As a result, in 1899, Congress passed the Height of Buildings Act, which restricted how tall buildings could be in DC. Maximum heights were based on the width of the street in front of the building. For most locations, that meant 110 feet was the limit (but 90 feet in residential neighborhoods). On avenues that were 160 feet wide, the height limit was 130 feet.

In 1910, the law was modified to allow buildings to be as tall as the street's width *plus* 20 feet, making the limit 130 feet in most commercial parts of the city. Buildings on certain parts of Pennsylvania Avenue were allowed to reach 160 feet.

The height limitation has made a huge impact on the city's appearance, creating an open, airy feeling and allowing structures such as the Capitol Building and the Washington Monument to be visible for miles.

The Senate Subway

DURING THE first century of its existence, the US Senate offices were mainly the senators' desks in the Senate Chamber. After that, some temporary solutions were found outside the Capitol Building, until finally in 1909, a Senate Office Building was constructed nearby to house the senators and their staffs.

Though it was only about a fifth of a mile from the Capitol, in the course of their workday, senators might have to make several trips back and forth between their offices and the Capitol. All that walking became quite tiresome, and it was decided that some kind of underground shuttle service should be installed to transport the senators back and forth.

The first system consisted of battery-powered yellow coaches that could each hold 10 passengers sitting on benches. These cars traveled at a top speed of 12 mph and made the trip forward in one direction and backward in the other direction—the coaches could not

★ **The Price of Doing Business** ★

If you wanted to run a business in Washington, DC, back in 1905, here's how much you would have to pay the government for a license:

Billiard halls: $12 per table, per year   Gasoline sellers: $5 per year

Bowling alleys: $12 per year   Ice cream parlors: $18 per year

Carriages for hire: $6 per year   Junk dealers: $40 per year

Circuses: $200 per day   Liquor stores: $800 per year

Fortune-tellers: $25 per year

★ **The Senate subway.**

Draw a Political Cartoon

POLITICAL CARTOONS are editorials—opinions—about current events, people in power, and the policies they make. These cartoons are usually both critical and funny at the same time. They use sarcasm or exaggeration, both in the drawing and in the words, to make a point.

American political cartoons have been around for as long as the government has. Many poke fun at the president, or at presidential candidates. In this activity you'll look at a couple of famous examples and create your own political cartoon.

One of the most famous Washington political cartoons was published in 1902. That year, while on a trip through Mississippi, President Theodore Roosevelt re-fused to shoot a bear that was in chains. *Washington Post* cartoonist Clifford Berryman drew a cartoon that immortalized that moment and inspired people to start associating Roosevelt with bears. That's how stuffed bears became known as teddy bears.

You'll Need
★ Paper
★ Pen

In political cartoons, famous people or places might be represented by animals, things, or ordinary people. For example, a man in a used car lot saying "I spent too much" might represent a politician, and the clunker car he bought might represent a project he funded.

Come up with a few different ideas and sketch them out. Take a look in the editorial section of your local newspaper for some examples of modern political cartoons.

★ Clifford Berryman's famous 1902 cartoon about Theodore Roosevelt.

be turned around. This system was replaced in 1912 by a double-line electric monorail system. The new cars, outfitted with wicker seats, could hold 18 passengers each. Each car made 225 trips a day (45 seconds each trip) when the Senate was in session.

In 1958, the construction of a new Senate Office Building a block farther away required the extension of the subway system. The old line was abandoned and a new tunnel built. The new subway cars had upholstered seats. As new buildings went up, the system was extended to reach them as well. Still in operation today, the subway runs in a 3,100-foot loop between buildings. The press once called this Senate subway the "shortest and most exclusive railway in the world."

★ Taken for Granted? ★

Another, lesser-known presidential memorial was dedicated in 1922—a statue of Ulysses S. Grant atop his horse was placed in Union Square, west of the US Capitol Building, near the Capitol Reflecting Pool. It is the largest equestrian monument in the United States at 252 feet long, 71 feet wide, and 44 feet high.

The Lincoln Memorial

EVEN WHILE President Lincoln was still alive, sculptors were trying to capture his image for posterity. The president sat for a talented young sculptor named Vinnie Ream in 1864–65. In 1866, after Lincoln's death, the 18-year-old Ream was hired to create a memorial statue, becoming the youngest artist and the first woman to be commissioned for a work of art by the US government. Her full-size marble statue of Lincoln stands in the Capitol Building.

In 1867, Congress authorized creation of the Lincoln Monument Association to establish a permanent memorial to the assassinated president. A sculptor named Clark Mills was hired to create a sculpture on the Capitol grounds. He envisioned a huge, multilevel, 36-person display, at the top center of which would be Lincoln signing the Emancipation Proclamation. This idea was never put into action.

The idea of a Lincoln monument went nowhere until 1900, when the Senate Park Commission was created to plan a park system for Washington. Commission members included architects, landscape architects, and a sculptor. The plan they published in 1902 called for a Lincoln memorial at the western end of the Mall, close to the Potomac. It would be placed on land that had not even existed a few decades before: the US Army Corps of Engineers dredged silt from the Potomac to deepen the river and used

★ **The Lincoln Memorial under construction in 1914.**

the material they dug out of the river to extend the land.

Congress created the Lincoln Memorial Commission in 1911, and the plan for a fitting tribute to the 16th president was on its way. Construction began in 1913. Henry Bacon was the architect; the sculptor of the giant statue inside the building was Daniel French. The memorial, which looks like an ancient Greek

Create a Walking Tour of Your Neighborhood

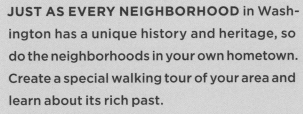

JUST AS EVERY NEIGHBORHOOD in Washington has a unique history and heritage, so do the neighborhoods in your own hometown. Create a special walking tour of your area and learn about its rich past.

We often get so used to our own neighborhoods that we hardly pay any attention to the details. How often do you pass by an old building with a hidden past? A school with a famous alumnus? A park with a really old tree? A house that's much older than you think? What interesting facts await discovery about places within walking distance of where you live?

You'll Need
★ Graph paper
★ Computer with Internet access
★ Notebook
★ Pen
★ Digital camera
★ Printer

Using graph paper, map out all or part of your neighborhood—at least a 4-block-by-4-block area. Mark each building on the map with a rectangle or appropriate shape. Do some research on your neighborhood—there are many possible resources. Many cities or counties offer online property searches that yield information about each building (such as the date built or the previous owners' names). Also check your local library or historical society for newspaper clippings, maps, photographs, and documents about your neighborhood's history.

Once your map is drawn, interview long-time neighborhood residents and ask them questions about what the area was like when they moved in. Do they have any old photographs or stories about certain buildings? Compile the information into a Walking Tour flyer by numbering the buildings or sites on the map for which you have information, picking logical starting and ending points for the tour. Then fill in the historical facts you've discovered for each tour stop and add digital photos that you took (and maybe scans of old photos, or of photos lent to you by neighbors, if available).

Now you're ready to conduct your tour!

---

temple, was completed in 1922. Its 36 Doric columns represent the 36 states in the Union in 1865, the year Lincoln died.

Robert Lincoln, the only surviving child of the former president, was present at the dedication ceremony on May 30, 1922. The keynote address at the dedication was delivered by the highly respected African American president of the Tuskegee Institute in Alabama, Dr. Robert Moton, yet the audience was segregated. Other speakers were the head of the Lincoln Memorial Commission (and Chief Justice of the Supreme Court) William Taft, and President Warren Harding.

★ **OPPOSITE: The 170-ton marble statue of Lincoln inside the memorial is 30 feet high.** Author's collection

Modern Washington

1930-Present

As the 20th century progressed, Washington, DC, grew into the cosmopolitan city it is today thanks in part to the many different transportation improvements. Highways and airports now make it easy to get to the city, and a modern subway system makes it easy to get around in it.

Airports

DURING THE early 20th century, Washington lagged behind other major cities in accommodating air travel. Two decades after Wilbur and Orville Wright took their historic first airplane flight, Hoover Field became the first airport in the DC area, opened in 1926 near the present site of the Pentagon.

★ **Christening of a new monoplane at Hoover Field in 1928.**

The airport attracted many people who were curious about flying. A popular company called the Potomac Flying Service was founded in April 1927. A Fairchild monoplane carried 1,500 passengers within its first 10 days of operation, and by November 1927, Potomac had carried 14,000 passengers (95 percent of whom were tourists) on flying tours of the area.

In 1927, Washington Airport opened next door to Hoover Field. The two airports merged in 1930 as Washington-Hoover Airport. Washington-Hoover's only runway was intersected by a street, so guards had to be posted to halt traffic while planes took off and landed, and pilots had to look out for electric wires and a nearby smokestack.

For more than 10 years, Congress debated about the need for a better airport for the nation's capital, but nothing was done. Finally, in 1938, President Franklin D. Roosevelt made the executive decision himself and announced that the new airport would be built about four and a half miles south of the city on mudflats along the Potomac River. Ground was broken for the National Airport (today known as Ronald Reagan Washington National Airport, after the nation's 40th president) in November 1938. It took nearly 20 million cubic yards of sand and gravel to make the messy site usable. The new four-runway airport opened in June 1941, and

344,000 passengers used the airport in its first year. By 1946, the number had risen to 1 million.

Washington National was considered to be quite an excellent, modern airport, but by the end of World War II it was clear that one airport wasn't enough for the city. In 1950 Congress authorized the construction of a second airport. A large site 26 miles west of Washington (and surrounded by farmland) was selected in 1958, and construction began on the first airport in the country designed for commercial jets. Dulles International Airport, named after the late Secretary of State John Foster Dulles, opened in 1962, and its centerpiece was the shining 600-foot-long terminal building designed by famous Finnish American architect Eero Saarinen. The main terminal was expanded in 1996 in a design that matched the original.

For many years National Airport remained the more widely used of the two. In 1975,

★ The iconic terminal building at Dulles Airport.

★ Presidential Flights ★

In 1943, Franklin Roosevelt became the first president to fly in an airplane while in office. Over the next 15 years, presidents flew in a variety of propeller planes until 1959, when President Dwight D. Eisenhower became the first to fly in a jet. President Kennedy was the first to fly in a jet built specially for presidential use—what would become known as Air Force One. The current Air Force One is housed at Andrews Air Force Base, a few miles east of Washington.

Dulles served 2.5 million passengers while National served 11.7 million. During the 1990s, Dulles flights increased dramatically, and it surpassed National Airport. In 2005, around 27 million passengers used Dulles. National Airport surpassed 20 million passengers for the first time in 2013.

Baseball in DC

THE FIRST major league baseball team in Washington, the Statesmen, began in 1891 as part of the American Association, one of the early leagues. In 1892, the club changed its name to the Senators and became part of the National League. The team was eliminated in 1899 when the National League shrank to eight teams, but was revived in 1901, as an American League team.

Following the 1960 season, the team moved to Minnesota and became the Twins. But Washington did not lose its team for good. In 1961, DC got a new Senators team as part of the expansion of the American League.

Though the Senators won the pennant and made it to the World Series in 1933, aside from that one-time success, they were perennially bad, usually ending their season at the bottom of the standings. As an old saying went, "First in war, first in peace, and last in the American League." In 1971, the team moved to Texas and became the Texas Rangers.

After a 33-year absence, baseball finally returned to DC in 1995, when the Montreal Expos moved to DC and became the Washington Nationals, a National League team. In five of the team's first six years, the Nationals finished in last place. They were looking very much like their predecessors, the Senators. But things turned around when, powered by new talent such as outfielder Bryce Harper, pitcher Stephen Strasburg, and outfielder Jayson Werth, the team finished third in 2011. In 2012 the Nationals had the best record in baseball, clinching a playoff spot—the first time a Washington team had finished in first place since 1933.

★ He Caught It ★

In 1910, President William Howard Taft began the tradition of throwing out a ball on baseball's Opening Day in Washington. After he threw the ball from the stands, players scrambled to catch the president's ball. This was still the case on Opening Day in 1952, when President Harry Truman threw out the first pitch. Washington Senators infielder Ted Lepcio, who was playing his first major league game, explained what happened that afternoon:

The president threw out the ball, and all the players, both teams are out there and the president throws the ball and everybody jumps around for it, and I was lucky, you had all those tall pitchers there bouncing around, and I ended up with the ball somehow. And I got ushered up to meet the president, President Truman, and went up there, and shook his hand, and that's it, and here we go. We haven't played an inning yet and here I've met the president of the United States.

Bonus Army Occupies Washington

SUFFERING FROM the effects of the Great Depression, World War I veterans wanted to receive their "bonus" payments that had been promised by Congress in 1924 to compensate for their lost work time while in the service. In 1931, Congress authorized payment of half of the amount due to them, but that was not enough. They wanted the other half.

Veterans around the country organized a pilgrimage to the nation's capital, intending to try to influence Congress to give them the rest of

★ **The Washington Senators at RFK Stadium on Opening Day 1971.**

the money due to them. Starting in May 1932, thousands of disgruntled World War I veterans descended upon the city, creating a "Bonus Army" of protestors. The ragtag group set up a camp southeast of Capitol Hill, as well as on property called Reservations A and B, located between Third and Sixth Streets and Pennsylvania and Missouri Avenues, which contained partly demolished buildings that were scheduled to be cleared soon.

By July, the House had voted in favor of the bonus bill, but the Senate voted it down. Now Congress was scheduled to adjourn for the summer. There was no point in staying in hot, muggy Washington over the summer, was there? The government wanted them out, and

★ **Bonus Army camp in Washington in 1932.**

offered free transportation home to the Bonus Army, and about a quarter of the veterans took the offer. The rest, however, remained. Rumors flew that many of the so-called veterans were actually Communists trying to cause trouble. President Herbert Hoover and the secretary of war were not pleased with the situation.

When attempts were made in late July by the local police to prevent members of the Bonus Army from occupying Reservations A and B, a riot occurred. According to an official report:

Many of the Bonus Army were walking about with clubs and bricks in their hands. This continued until the middle of the afternoon, with continuous talk about attacking the police and driving them out. Some lawfully inclined veterans attempted to calm others, but made no impression. Finally the mob of bonus marchers again attacked the police with bricks, lumps of concrete, and iron bars. Two of the bonus marchers were shot by police who had been set upon and were in danger of their lives. The entire mob became hostile and riotous. It was apparent that a pitched battle on a large scale might start at any moment. Practically the entire police force of the city were called from their posts and assembled at this point, but they were outnumbered 10 or 15 to 1.

The US Army was called in, and at 7 PM the Bonus Army was told they'd have to evacuate their camp. The scene was one of chaos and confusion as several fires were set, first by the retreating marchers and then by the army. Before long, the entire camp was in flames, and the Bonus Army had dispersed completely.

More Jobs for DC

CITIES ACROSS the United States suffered great economic losses during the Great Depression. Washington was slightly better off than most cities, thanks to President Franklin Roosevelt's policies. Roosevelt's New Deal created many federal, Washington-based agencies to help get the nation out of the Great Depression, agencies such as the Works Progress Administration, National Recovery Administration, Social Security Administration, and Civilian Conservation Corps. With this expanded role of the federal government came thousands of jobs, a great many of them to the city of Washington. In 1933, there were 63,000 federal jobs in Washington. Within two years, that number had jumped to 93,000. By 1940, there were 166,000 federal jobs in Washington.

The Jefferson Memorial and the Cherry Tree Controversy

THE JEFFERSON Memorial Commission was formed in 1936 to look into creating a permanent memorial to the country's third president.

When it was announced in 1937 that the Tidal Basin had been selected as the site for this new building, opponents who looked at the original plans for the memorial claimed that most of the cherry trees located there would be lost. Months passed, and a compromise was reached. The new design relocated the memorial to the south part of the basin, where it would have a lesser impact on the cherry trees. Opponents were still not satisfied.

On November 17, 1938, a group of 50 women protested in front of the White House, and the next day, 150 women showed up at the Tidal Basin, led by Eleanor Patterson, the owner/editor of the *Washington Times-Herald*. The protestors symbolically chained themselves to a tree,

★ BELOW: **President Roosevelt lays the cornerstone for the Jefferson Memorial in 1939.**

★ RIGHT: **The Jefferson Memorial.**

and took shovels away from workers removing trees. The protest was eventually disbanded peacefully.

Roosevelt claimed that only 88 trees would be lost, but the opponents said the number was much higher. Roosevelt also promised that whatever was lost would be replaced with new trees elsewhere along the Tidal Basin. The opposition seemed to die down, and when it came time for the groundbreaking in December, there were no protests.

The memorial opened on April 13, 1943, the 200th anniversary of Jefferson's birthday. Visitors are always struck by the beauty of the site and all the cherry trees surrounding the memorial.

The US Supreme Court Gets a Home

THE US Supreme Court held its first session in the nation's first capital, New York City, back in 1790. In 1791, it moved to the new capital, Philadelphia. When the federal government moved to Washington in 1800, no provisions had been made for the Court, so Congress agreed to let the Court meet in the Capitol.

Over the next 130 years, the US Supreme Court heard all types of important cases in six different places within the Capitol Building, including a room in the basement. William

★ **The Supreme Court building in 1936.**

Howard Taft was the major force behind the Court getting its own home. He first began pushing the idea in 1912 when he was president, and continued the cause when he became chief justice of the Supreme Court in 1921. Through his efforts, Congress agreed to

107

spend up to $9.7 million on construction of the new building, and famous architect Cass Gilbert was chosen to design the Court's new home. Taft told Gilbert to create "a building of dignity and importance suitable for its use as the permanent home of the Supreme Court of the United States." His classical Corinthian design features rows of columns.

In October 1932, two years after Taft had died, the cornerstone was laid for the new Supreme Court Building, located at First Street NE. A thousand freight cars full of Vermont marble were shipped in for the exterior walls. The Court first met in the new building in October 1935. Since then, the words "Supreme Court" have become synonymous with the image of the building.

Marian Anderson's Lincoln Memorial Concert

MARIAN ANDERSON was a world famous African American opera singer who had performed at the Paris Opera House in 1935 and Carnegie Hall and the White House in 1936. Starting that same year, she sang an annual concert at Howard University in Washington. But before long her audience had outgrown that space and needed a bigger hall, so in January 1939, her manager and Howard University asked the Daughters of the American Revolution, a patriotic organization, if she could use the DAR's Constitution Hall, the city's largest auditorium, with 4,000 seats.

However, at the time the DAR was an all-white organization, and Washington was still a segregated city. Blacks who attended events at Constitution Hall had to sit in a separate section of the auditorium, away from white attendees. The DAR rejected Anderson's request, just as it had rejected a request for the black singer Paul Robeson to perform there in 1930. In February 1939 the District of Columbia Board of Education also declined a request to use the large auditorium of Central High School, a white public school, for the performance.

After the DAR rejected Anderson, a large number of local churches and organizations—65 black groups and 32 white groups—banded together to form the Marian Anderson Citizens Committee. They notified Eleanor Roosevelt of the situation, and on February 25, 1939, Mrs. Roosevelt resigned from the Daughters of the American Revolution, saying, "I am in complete disagreement with the attitude taken in refusing Constitution Hall to a great artist. You set an example which seems to me unfortunate, and I feel obligated to send in to you my resignation."

Franklin and Eleanor Roosevelt and the committee worked together to set up a free outdoor concert at the Lincoln Memorial. They asked Secretary of the Interior Harold Ickes to allow the concert. Ickes, a former official in the Chicago chapter of the NAACP, was happy to oblige.

A total of 75,000 people attended the landmark concert on April 9, which included Anderson's renditions of "America the Beautiful" and "Ave Maria." The 30-minute performance was also broadcast over the radio and heard by hundreds of thousands of people across the country. In introducing Anderson, Ickes said, "Genius knows no color line." What had begun as a discouraging episode in race relations wound up as a triumph.

Just a few years later, in 1942, the DAR invited Marian Anderson to perform a wartime benefit concert at Constitution Hall, and in 1953, she performed there in front of an unsegregated audience.

The Pentagon

WITH WORLD WAR II threatening to engulf the United States, the War Department (precursor to the Department of Defense) needed more room to house military staff. The Department already occupied 17 buildings in DC, and rather than build several more small buildings, it would be more efficient to create a central location for all military and war-related personnel to be housed.

In July 1941, General Brehon Somervell had plans drawn up for a massive, three-story building that could house 40,000 people. Con-

gress quickly set aside money and construction started in September. By early December there were 4,000 men working daily at the site, across the Potomac in Arlington, Virginia, near Arlington National Cemetery. Five roads surrounded the 67-acre site, so the building was designed with five sides—a pentagon.

After the Japanese attack on Pearl Harbor sparked the United States' entry into World

★ **Marian Anderson gives her concert from the steps of the Lincoln Memorial in 1939.**

War II, the planned height of the Pentagon was increased to five stories, for a total of 6.6 million square feet of space—three times as much as the Empire State Building. Completion became more urgent, and now there were 16,000 men working on the construction project. On April 30, 1942, the first government employees moved in, and by June there were 15,000 people working in the finished part of the building.

The entire building was completed on January 15, 1943. It has over 7,000 windows, 131 stairways, and 17.5 miles of corridors. The parking lot can hold 8,700 vehicles. Even though it is in Arlington, Virginia, mail addressed to one of the Pentagon's six different zip codes must say "Washington, DC."

The Beltway and Suburbs

THE DEVELOPMENT of Washington's suburbs began in the 1800s in the areas right next to the capital, places that would be easy enough to travel to and from. The conversion from horse-drawn cars to electric streetcars was a major improvement. All the trolley lines in Washington were privately owned. Developers who were building homes and promoting certain suburbs built their own trolley lines to make it more enticing for people to buy their properties.

By the end of the 19th century, one of the places that was being developed was Chevy Chase, Maryland, which was on the border of DC and Maryland. The Chevy Chase Land Company developed 1,700 acres of land and built bridges and a streetcar line. It took 35 minutes to get to downtown Washington by streetcar. The last Washington streetcar ran in 1962.

An excellent railway station and two modern airports helped improve access to the nation's capital, but there was still one mode of transportation that lagged behind: the automobile. There were plenty of roads through which to access the city, but no major highway nearby to provide easier access from the many suburbs. The idea of a highway "ring" around the capital was proposed as the best way to provide the people living in various surrounding suburbs with access to the city.

This highway was first planned in 1950, and construction began in 1955 in Maryland and 1958 in Virginia. The first segment to open was a 1.6-mile portion in Montgomery County, Maryland, in 1957. Construction continued for seven more years, and the final link of the Beltway was opened on August 17, 1964.

All in all, the Capital Beltway is 63.8 miles long, with 22.1 miles in Virginia, and 41.7 miles in Maryland. It was originally six lanes wide for 49 miles and four lanes wide for 14 miles. By the late 1960s the Beltway was handling about 80,000 cars per day. Today the highway handles up to 225,000 vehicles per day, resulting in big

Search for Your Family in the National Archives Records

THE NATIONAL ARCHIVES Building opened in 1935 on Pennsylvania Avenue, built to store the nation's most important federal records. The Archives maintains a comprehensive collection of all kinds of government documents, including many that can be of great help to people wanting to research their family tree.

One of the Archives' best genealogy resources is the Federal Census. Taken every 10 years, the census counts the population of the United States and records data about the people who live in this country. Originally census takers went door to door, asking questions about the names, ages, occupations, birthplaces, citizenship, and other information about each member of the household. Today, most people respond via questionnaires that the government mails to every household in the country.

The complete census data is officially released to the public 72 years after it was taken, so the 1940 census became available in 2012. According to Ancestry.com, 87 percent of Americans can find at least one relative in the 1940 census. In this activity, you'll explore the 1940 census and see what you can find about your family.

You'll Need
★ Device with Internet connection (the bigger the screen, the better)
★ Pen and paper
★ Printer (optional)
★ Family members to question

Get as much information as possible from your parents, grandparents, great-uncles or great-aunts, or anyone who might know where your family in the United States lived in 1940. If you know their exact address, that can be very helpful, but just knowing their town, exact names, and approximate ages of the people in the household can be enough as well. Keep in mind that last names in the census were not always spelled correctly, and first names were whatever the head of the household gave out, which sometimes meant nicknames—a great-grandparent you always knew as Elizabeth might have been referred to as Lizzie, Beth, Betty, or Elsie.

There are several websites with free access to the 1940 census. The site 1940census .archives.gov is the official site, but searching may be easier at familysearch.org or other sites where you can use names to search, rather than just addresses.

What you will see when you click into the census info page for your family may take a few minutes to decipher, but once you understand it you can also look at the names of your family's neighbors, recorded just before and after your family. Sometimes these names will sound familiar from old family stories, or will be recognized by the older members of your family.

The information you obtain through the 1940 census records can help you go back further into your family's American past. With the facts that you gather, you can then try to find your relatives in the 1930, 1920, 1910, and 1900 censuses, depending on when they arrived in this country. Keep in mind that especially with immigrants and in big cities, not everyone who lived here was counted. So, you may find your family in one census but not in others. It doesn't mean they weren't in the US, only that the census taker missed them or they didn't answer the door.

The information you find in census records can also help you locate other information, including immigration records, birth/marriage/death records, and naturalization records. Indexes for these are also available through the National Archives.

traffic delays. Parts of the Beltway have since been widened (including 21 miles in Virginia from six to eight lanes), but even this is not enough to handle the great volume of vehicles. Recent studies rated Washington's traffic congestion the worst of any city in the country; DC drivers spend an average of 67 hours a year stuck in traffic. Washington also has the longest rush hours of any city, with seven hours of the day being considered part of the rush hour.

The Beltway includes two bridge crossings over the Potomac River. Construction on the 5,900-foot-long Woodrow Wilson Bridge (crossing the river at Alexandria, Virginia) began in 1958 and the bridge opened in 1961. The 1,400-foot-long Legion Bridge crosses the river near Cabin John, Maryland, and opened in 1962.

With the interstate highway system beginning in the 1950s, and then the Metro subway system beginning in the 1970s (see page 116), more and more people who worked in DC began to move to the surrounding towns. Of the 312,000 workers in Washington as of 2013, getting to work took 20 percent of them 45 minutes or longer. These commuters come from all over Virginia and Maryland, and even farther. But 75 percent of the people who live in Washington also work in Washington, which is a very high number compared to most other cities.

★ **The Washington Beltway in Silver Spring, Maryland, in 2001.**

Civil Rights March

Protest marches in Washington, DC, date back to the late 19th century. Up to the mid-20th century, the largest of these involved about 50,000 people, and most of them are not much remembered today. All that changed during the 1960s, a volatile time in the nation's history. Nineteen sixty-three was a turning point: President Kennedy had just introduced the Civil Rights Act, and civil rights activist Medgar Evers had been murdered in Jackson, Mississippi, in June.

The March on Washington for Jobs and Freedom in 1963 attracted about 250,000 people, including about 60,000 whites. It was timed so that it coincided with the 100th anniversary of the Emancipation Proclamation. Organizing the march was a massive undertaking. More than 2,000 chartered buses brought marchers in from all over the country, and volunteers made 80,000 boxed lunches to feed the crowd. There were 5,900 DC police officers on duty, along with an additional 6,000 soldiers and members of the National Guard.

Marchers carried signs demanding equal rights and integrated schools. The highlight

★ LEFT: **Civil rights marchers in Washington, August 1963.**

★ BELOW: **Program for the March on Washington.**

MARCH ON WASHINGTON
FOR JOBS AND FREEDOM
AUGUST 28, 1963

LINCOLN MEMORIAL PROGRAM

1.	The National Anthem	Led by Marian Anderson.
2.	Invocation	The Very Rev. Patrick O'Boyle, Archbishop of Washington.
3.	Opening Remarks	A. Philip Randolph, Director March on Washington for Jobs and Freedom.
4.	Remarks	Dr. Eugene Carson Blake, Stated Clerk, United Presbyterian Church of the U.S.A.; Vice Chairman, Commission on Race Relations of the National Council of Churches of Christ in America.
5.	Tribute to Negro Women Fighters for Freedom Daisy Bates Diane Nash Bevel Mrs. Medgar Evers Mrs. Herbert Lee Rosa Parks Gloria Richardson	Mrs. Medgar Evers
6.	Remarks	John Lewis, National Chairman, Student Nonviolent Coordinating Committee.
7.	Remarks	Walter Reuther, President, United Automobile, Aerospace and Agricultural Implement Workers of America, AFL-CIO; Chairman, Industrial Union Department, AFL-CIO.
8.	Remarks	James Farmer, National Director, Congress of Racial Equality.
9.	Selection	Eva Jessye Choir
10.	Prayer	Rabbi Uri Miller, President Synagogue Council of America.
11.	Remarks	Whitney M. Young, Jr., Executive Director, National Urban League.
12.	Remarks	Mathew Ahmann, Executive Director, National Catholic Conference for Interracial Justice.
13.	Remarks	Roy Wilkins, Executive Secretary, National Association for the Advancement of Colored People.
14.	Selection	Miss Mahalia Jackson
15.	Remarks	Rabbi Joachim Prinz, President American Jewish Congress.
16.	Remarks	The Rev. Dr. Martin Luther King, Jr., President, Southern Christian Leadership Conference.
17.	The Pledge	A Philip Randolph
18.	Benediction	Dr. Benjamin E. Mays, President, Morehouse College.

"WE SHALL OVERCOME"

of the protest was the famous "I Have a Dream" speech by Dr. Martin Luther King Jr. in front of the Lincoln Memorial. There were other speakers, too, including 23-year-old John Lewis, who was chairman of an organization called the Student Nonviolent Coordinating Committee and the youngest person to speak that day. His inspiring speech began, "We march today for jobs and freedom, but we have nothing to be proud of. For hundreds and thousands of our brothers are not here. For they are receiving starvation wages, or no wages at all."

The march was a historic moment and a turning point in the civil rights movement. In July 1964, President Lyndon Johnson signed the Civil Rights Act into law. The law made discrimination in employment and in public places illegal, and provided for integration of public schools.

There have been other civil rights marches since then, including 1995's "Million Man March" on Washington, organized by a minister and activist named Louis Farrakhan. Somewhere between 400,000 and 800,000 black men attended this rally in support of equality and overcoming racial stereotypes.

The Vote and Home Rule

THOUGH WASHINGTON, DC, has always been incredibly important to our nation, for more than 150 years, its own citizens had very limited rights. The city was still run by a Board of Commissioners appointed by the president. And not only were DC residents unable to elect their own local leaders, they also were not even allowed to vote in presidential elections.

ACTIVITY

Write Your Own Dream Speech

WHEN DR. MARTIN LUTHER KING JR. spoke before the 250,000 people gathered in Washington on that August day in 1963, he made history. His "I Have a Dream" speech, as it became known, inspired millions across the country to fight for civil rights. In the speech, he shared several dreams he had for America, including the dream that his four children would one day "live in a nation where they will not be judged by the color of their skin but by the content of their character," that the state of Mississippi would be "transformed into an oasis of freedom and justice," and that one day in Georgia "the sons of slaves and the sons of slave owners will be able to sit together at the table of brotherhood." You can find the entire speech here: www.archives.gov/press/exhibits/dream-speech.pdf.

Look at the speech and especially the section where Dr. King talks about his six dreams for a better future. Notice how he used concrete examples of people and places that make his speech both touching and rousing. If you were to write your own version of a "dream" speech today, what issue would you write about? What are the problems plaguing your town, your state, or the country as a whole? What are your dreams for the future? Write a brief lead-in to the topic and then explain your six dreams. Whether it's about civil rights, poverty, hunger, war, or some other issue, use words that describe specific examples to make your dream speech more powerful.

For years there was a growing movement to change this. Finally, in May 1949, the Senate passed, without a single dissenting vote, an act to bring "home rule" to Washington. President Harry Truman sent a letter to the Speaker of the House in July 1949 urging the House to pass the bill as well, saying,

It is little short of fantastic that the Congress of the United States should—as it now does—devote a substantial percentage of its time to acting as a city council for the District of Columbia. During the past two years, during which it was confronted with many major problems of national and international importance, the Congress has had to find time to deal with such District matters as parking lots, the regulation of barbers, the removal of street obstructions, and the establishment of a Metropolitan Police Force Band, to name only a few.

The bill never came to a vote in the House, and the issue was stalled. That same year, a senator from West Virginia introduced a constitutional amendment that would give Washington electoral votes and its citizens the right to vote in national elections. Again, nothing happened, and over the next decade more attempts were made. The amendment was finally proposed by Congress in June 1960, and ratified by on March 29, 1961. It gave Washington, DC, the same number of electoral votes as the smallest state: two. Washingtonians could now vote in presidential elections . . . but still could not elect their own government.

President John F. Kennedy said, "Ratification of the 23rd amendment giving the residents of the District of Columbia the right to vote in Presidential elections by the required 38 States is a major step in the right direction. . . . It is equally important that residents of the District of Columbia have the right to select the officials who govern the District. I am hopeful that the Congress, spurred by the adoption of the 23rd Amendment, will act favorably on legislative proposals to be recommended by the Administration providing the District of Columbia the right of home rule."

Still nothing happened.

When Washington voted in the 1964 election, the results were overwhelmingly in favor of the Democratic candidate, Lyndon Johnson (85.5 percent) over Republican Barry Goldwater (14.5 percent). Johnson won there by a bigger margin than anywhere else in the country, perhaps in part because he pledged to finally get home rule for Washington.

On February 2, 1965, President Johnson delivered a special message to Congress:

The restoration of home rule to the citizens of the District of Columbia must no longer be delayed. Our Federal, State, and local governments

One of the most memorable figures in Washington's local political history was Marion Barry Jr., an African American civil rights activist from Mississippi, who moved to Washington in 1965 to found a chapter of a group called the Student Nonviolent Coordinating Committee. Before long, he entered politics, winning a seat on the city council. He ran for mayor in 1978 and was elected. Barry won reelection in 1982, and won a third term in 1986. His career came to a halt in 1990, however, when he was caught in an FBI sting using crack cocaine and sentenced to six months in prison for drug possession.

Once he was released, Barry ran for city council again, using the slogan "He may not be perfect, but he's perfect for DC." He won, and then ran for mayor again in 1994, and won. Though he retired from politics in 1998, he came back again in 2004, winning another term on the city council. Despite being plagued by run-ins with the law, he won reelection in 2008, and again in 2012. He died in 2014 while still in office.

rest on the principle of democratic representation—the people elect those who govern them. We cherish the credo declared by our forefathers: No taxation without representation. We know full well that men and women give the most of themselves when they are permitted to attack problems which directly affect them.

Yet the citizens of the District of Columbia, at the very seat of the government created by our Constitution, have no vote in the government of their city. They are taxed without representation. They are asked to assume the responsibilities of citizenship while denied one of its basic rights. No major capital in the free world is in a comparable condition of disenfranchisement.

Once again, Congress stalled. In fact, the Senate passed bills providing some form of home rule six times between 1948 and 1966, and six times the bill died before it could be voted on in the House. In 1967, the Board of Commissioners was finally replaced with a mayor and city council—but these leaders would be appointed by the president. (Washingtonians did, however, win the right to elect their own school board.) Appropriately enough, the first mayor who was appointed under this new law was named Walter Washington.

Three years later, DC residents won the right to have a nonvoting representative in the House. And finally, in 1973, Congress passed the District of Columbia Self-Government and Governmental Reorganization Act, a.k.a. the Home Rule Act, which gave DC residents the right to elect their own government. The next year, Washingtonians approved the measure in a referendum. When it came time for the first mayoral election in November 1974, Walter Washington won another term as mayor, this time as the people's choice.

In 1978, Congress passed the Voting Rights Amendment, which gave DC voting representation in Congress, but the amendment never became law, because it was not ratified by the required minimum of 38 states.

The Washington Metro

WASHINGTON'S LAYOUT makes it fine for driving, but parking is another story. Restrictions due to the Mall and the many museums, parks, and government buildings make it nearly impossible to find a parking space near any of the major attractions. A subway system is the perfect way to move large numbers of people efficiently.

In 1952 Congress passed the National Capital Planning Act, which laid the groundwork for such a system in DC. Other cities in the United States, such as Boston and New York, had already had subways for many decades. It was time for the nation's capital to finally have its own subway system.

After many years of planning and discussion, the Washington Metrorail system, or Metro, finally broke ground on December 9, 1969, at Judiciary Square, before a crowd of 1,500 people including numerous government officials. In 1972, as construction continued, 300 Metro cars were ordered. Finally, on March 27, 1976, Metrorail service began. It was an exciting time in the city's history. More than 50,000 people rode for free along the original 4.2-mile Red Line route, consisting of five stations.

Metrorail originally ran only from 6 AM to 8 PM on weekdays and was closed on weekends, which was fine for most commuters but meant that DC visitors still had to take taxi cabs during late evening hours.

The system continued to grow. In 1977, the 18-station Blue Line opened, and more stations and lines were added in the years that followed. In 1978 Metro's hours of operation were extended to midnight. Today, the system serves a population of 3.4 million and consists of 86 stations along 106 miles of track in DC, Virginia, and Maryland. On Inauguration Weekend 2009, a record was set with spectators taking 2.6 million trips over three days, and on July 4, 2010, Metrorail set a new single-day ridership record of 598,898 trips.

★ **Metro Center Station under construction in 1973.**

★ ABOVE: **Metro Center Station today.**

★ RIGHT: **Giant pandas at the National Zoo.**

The Metro, with its fast, frequent, quiet service and its clean stations, is a true Washington icon.

The Gift of Pandas

RELATIONS BETWEEN the United States and China were tense during the Cold War era. When President Richard Nixon visited China in 1972, it was seen as the dawn of a new and more open relationship between the two countries. China's leader, Mao Zedong, offered to donate two rare giant pandas to the United States. Nixon offered two musk ox (which are native to North America) in return.

The pair of young pandas, a female named Ling-Ling and a male named Hsing-Hsing, arrived at the National Zoo in April 1972. In the years that followed, the panda pair attracted millions of visitors.

Four panda cubs were born to the couple, but sadly, none survived past the first week. Ling-Ling died in 1992, and Hsing-Hsing in 1999. A new pair of pandas arrived in 2000, Tian Tian and Mei Xiang, and they had two surviving cubs, Bao Bao and Tai Shan.

Diplomats Everywhere!

BECAUSE WASHINGTON is the nation's capital, it is home to more than 175 foreign embassies. These embassies serve not only as their countries' official presence in the United States; they also serve as a resource for their citizens who are visiting or living in this country, and they are visited by foreign leaders. Each embassy's staff is led by an ambassador, assisted by a variety of diplomats, including attachés, counselors, and secretaries.

Dozens of embassies are located in former mansions in a neighborhood formerly known as Millionaire's Row, now called Embassy Row. More than 45 embassies are located along Massachusetts Avenue and another 12 are along New Hampshire Avenue.

The size of the staff depends on the size of the country, the closeness, importance, and complexity of its relationship with the United States, and the number of its citizens living in or visiting the United States. Neighboring Canada's embassy has a staff of more than 135 diplomats, while Mexico has at least 75. The

Make a Cut-and-Cover Metro Tunnel

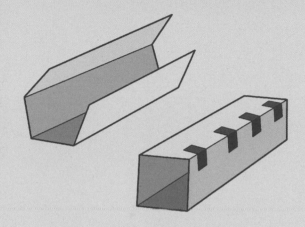

THERE ARE A FEW DIFFERENT WAYS to create subway tunnels. In places that require deep tunnels, or where the tunnel must be dug through rock, tunnel boring machines are used to burrow horizontally through the ground. Another option is the cut-and-cover method, which involves digging a trench, creating a tunnel, and covering the rest of the trench back up again. Much of the Washington Metro was built using the cut-and-cover method. Because of the obvious disruption to the street above, this work must be done as quickly as possible. What is the ideal shape for a metro tunnel? In this activity you will create a cut-and-cover tunnel of your own and figure out the answer.

You'll Need
★ Paper towel tube
★ Piece of cardboard of similar thickness, about 8 inches by 14 inches
★ Electrical tape
★ Trowel

You'll test cardboard tunnels of two different shapes, circular and square. For the circular tunnel, simply use the tube from the center of a paper towel roll. For the square tunnel, find a piece of cardboard

about the same thickness as the paper towel tube. Fold the long side of the piece of cardboard in half, then in half again. Unfold and bend the edges together to create a rectangular tube. Secure the edges with electrical tape.

On a sandy beach or in your yard, dig two parallel trenches slightly longer than the length of the tubes, about 1 foot apart and 6 inches deep. Lay each of the tubes into a trench and then cover them both with about 3 inches of sand or dirt. Press down lightly on the soil or sand to make sure it is compacted. Now walk back and forth a few times on top of your covered trenches. Carefully dig up your tunnels and examine them. Which shape held up better?

★ **The Prince of Wales (right) at the French Embassy in 1919.**

small European country of Monaco has only four diplomats on staff, while Russia, a large and influential power, has 118.

Foreign diplomats must be treated according to the Vienna Convention on Diplomatic Relations, adopted in 1961, which says, "The person of a diplomatic agent shall be inviolable. He shall not be liable to any form of arrest or detention. The receiving State shall treat him with due respect and shall take all appropriate steps to prevent any attack on his person, freedom, or dignity. . . . A diplomatic agent shall enjoy immunity from the criminal jurisdiction of the receiving State. He shall also enjoy immunity from its civil and administrative jurisdiction."

The presence of so many thousands of diplomats from all over the world gives Washington a unique international flavor and exposure to all kinds of cultures and traditions.

Lobbyist City

As THE nation's capital, Washington, DC, has always been a government city. Of the more than 740,000 jobs in Washington today, 203,000 (27 percent) are federal jobs. And that is just people who work directly for the federal government. It doesn't even count thousands more who perform services for the government, such as the printing of reports and upkeep of government buildings and parks.

There are also thousands of people in the city who are *lobbyists*—people whose job it is to try to get Congress to vote in a certain way on a certain issue. The term "lobbyist" came into use because these people would hang around in the lobby of a legislative building, trying to meet and greet (and influence) lawmakers on one subject or another. The lobby of the US Capitol was specifically designed so that, according to architect Benjamin Latrobe, "The Lobby of the House is so separated from it that those who retire to it cannot see and probably will not distinctly hear what is going forward in it."

Most often, lobbyists are not people acting on their own. They are highly paid professionals who represent a large group of people, such as the gun lobby (representing manufacturers and citizens in favor of limiting restrictions on purchasing and owning guns). Lobbyists in Washington also represent the tobacco industry, the defense industry, pharmaceutical companies, and the mining industry, to name just a few.

Lobbying was unregulated until 1946, when Congress passed the Federal Regulation of Lobbying Act. The 1995 Lobbying Disclosure Act put even more strict regulations on lobbying. Even so, lobbyists spend more than $3 billion every year trying to influence Congress. As of 2013, there were more than 12,000 lobbyists in the city.

New Memorials

FOR OVER 40 years, the Jefferson Memorial stood as the last memorial to have been built in Washington. Then, in 1980, Congress authorized a nonprofit group called the Vietnam Veterans Memorial Fund to fund and build a memorial to the men and women who lost their lives in the Vietnam conflict, which had officially ended five years earlier.

The Vietnam Veterans Memorial was to be located north of the Lincoln Memorial at the western end of the Mall. There was an open competition in 1981, and 1,421 designs were submitted. The winner was a 20-year-old American college student named Maya Lin. Her design consisted of two 246-foot-long sunken black stone walls etched with names.

Not everyone embraced this winning entry. A letter to President Reagan signed by 27 Republican congressmen expressed their concerns: "We feel this design makes a political statement of shame and dishonor, rather than an expression of our national pride." In January 1982, Secretary of the Interior James Watt demanded changes be incorporated into the design to satisfy the critics. A sculpture of three soldiers and an American flag were added to the design, and the memorial was allowed to go forward.

Ground was broken in March 1982, and by November the Vietnam Veterans Memo-

★ **The Vietnam Veterans Memorial.** Author's collection

rial was finished and dedicated. The memorial lists the names of each of the 58,000 men and women who died during the conflict, chronologically from 1959 to 1975. It is visited by nearly 4 million people each year.

Other Washington memorials which followed were the Korean War Memorial in 1995, the Franklin Delano Roosevelt Memorial in 1997, the World War II Memorial in 2004, and the Martin Luther King, Jr. Memorial in 2011.

At of the time of this writing, a memorial to President Dwight D. Eisenhower was being planned, to be located at the base of Capitol Hill.

The Terror Attacks of 9/11

ON THE morning of September 11, 2001, terrorists hijacked four airplanes with the intent to kill Americans and cause major damage to landmark buildings in the United States. Two planes hit the towers of the World Trade Center in New York, causing their collapse and killing over 2,500 people.

Another crashed on the ground in Pennsylvania after passengers tried to take back control of the plane from the terrorists. All the people on board this plane, which may have been bound for the White House, died in the crash.

The final plane, American Airlines Flight 77, had taken off from Dulles Airport and was over Kentucky when the hijackers took control of the plane and turned it back toward Washington. They crashed the plane into the Pentagon at 9:37 AM, a little over an hour after takeoff. It was a scene of chaos at the nation's defense headquarters, as flames swept through the southwest portion of the building. All 64 people on the plane died, along with 124 who were working in the building. The damaged section of the Pentagon (including 400,000 square feet that had to be completely demolished) was rebuilt by September 2002.

Segway City

WASHINGTON IS one of the nation's top tourist attractions, but the various sites are spread over a large area. While the Metro helps tourists get around, Washington is still very much a walking city.

In 2001, a new invention called the Segway Personal Transporter appeared. This one-person, two-wheeled, self-balancing electric vehicle seemed promising for use in a city such as Washington. In 2012, Segway started offering tours of the Smithsonian complex on the Mall. The DC Police Department also uses Segways, as does the Parking Enforcement Department.

Because Segways are not considered motor vehicles, they follow the same rules as bicycles. In some areas of the city they are allowed on both roadways and sidewalks, but downtown, because there are so many pedestrians on the sidewalks, they can only be used on the street.

Earthquake!

ON AUGUST 23, 2011, a 5.8 magnitude earthquake occurred in Mineral, Virginia, 84 miles southwest of Washington, DC. The tremor was felt in Washington and all up and down the East Coast; because the area is so populous, it was felt by more people than any other earthquake in United States history.

Interestingly, the first Washingtonians to sense the quake were animals at the National Zoo, many of whom actually detected it several seconds before the tremor hit. There were no injuries in Washington, but the White House and the Capitol were evacuated, along with many office buildings. Three decorative carvings called *finials* fell off the spires of the Washington National Cathedral, and the Washington Monument was damaged, developing 150 cracks. The government shut it down for repairs. It reopened in May 2014.

The Future of Washington

OVER THE course of two centuries in our nation's capital, presidents have come and gone, political parties have risen and fallen, and thousands of laws have been passed. Through it all, good and bad, Washington has remained one of the most important and amazing cities in the world.

Created from nothing, it has become the center of our democracy and a worldwide symbol of freedom itself. Its beauty, accessibility, and cultural and historic significance make it a popular destination for tourists—19 million a year—and it is home to more than 660,000 residents.

Washington today is a lively, growing, world-class city. It belongs to all the people of the United States, and we will all share in its bright and exciting future.

Be an Engineer

AFTER AN EARTHQUAKE shook Washington in 2011, engineers were called on to quickly examine many of the city's buildings for damage. The stiffer the structure, the more damage can be caused. Though you might think a taller building would be more likely to be damaged, it's the shorter, older, and more rigid ones that may suffer most, while a taller, steel-framed building is more flexible and sways. In recent years, stricter building codes have resulted in new buildings that are better able to resist the shock of an earthquake, but older ones are still vulnerable.

You can be a building engineer, too.

You'll Need
★ Pad of graph paper
★ Digital camera
★ Measuring tape (the longer the better)
★ Pencil or pen

Pick a local building that is at least partly made of some kind of stone—your home, your school, your church, or your library, for example. Measure the building as best you can, and then draw an outline of it on graph paper to a scale of your choosing—for example, 1 foot of the building could equal 1 square of graph paper. Walk around the outside of the building and look for cracks or *spalls* (areas where concrete or stone has chipped away). Use the tape measure to figure out where the problem is so you can mark it on your graph paper with an X.

Now take a photo of the damaged area and measure how big it is. Mark this on your graph paper next to the X, along with what the type of problem is. You may also note discoloration or staining, which could be a sign of water leakage (which can cause more serious damage in the future). Most buildings, especially older ones, will have some minor cracks and spalls that are usually nothing serious.

Engineers do exactly this for buildings and bridges regularly, compiling their findings, including lots of photos, into a report. They decide which problems are serious and which are minor, and recommend how to repair them. In the case of earthquake damage, they may recommend measures to strengthen and repair damaged parts of a building (as they did for the Washington Monument), or they may recommend the building be demolished if the damage is too severe.

★ Acknowledgments ★

Thanks to family and friends for their continued support, and thanks to the folks at Chicago Review Press for continuing to allow me to be a part of this high-quality line of children's books.

★ Resources ★

Books to Read

Aragon, Catherine. *Mission Washington, D.C.: A Scavenger Hunt Adventure*. Aragon Books: New York, 2014

House, Katherine L. *The White House for Kids*. Chicago: Chicago Review Press, 2014.

Miller, Brandon Marie. *George Washington for Kids*. Chicago: Chicago Review Press, 2007.

Ogintz, Eileen. *The Kid's Guide to Washington, DC*. New York: Globe Pequot Press, 2013.

Panchyk, Richard. *Keys to American History*. Chicago: Chicago Review Press, 2009

Panchyk, Richard. *Our Supreme Court*. Chicago: Chicago Review Press, 2006.

Reis, Ronald A. *The US Congress for Kids*. Chicago: Chicago Review Press, 2014.

Sasek, Miroslav. *This Is Washington, D.C.* New York: Rizzoli Publishers, 2011.

Websites to Visit

Official website of the Smithsonian Institution
www.si.edu

National Park Service website detailing all of DC's national parks, historic sites, memorials, and monuments
www.nps.gov/state/dc/index.htm

Homepage of the Washington Metro, providing schedules and trip planners for DC's subway system and buses
www.wmata.com

The official tourism site of Washington, DC
http://washington.org/

The Capitol's online visitor center
www.visitthecapitol.gov

Library of Congress website, where you can search for historic and present-day images of Washington, DC
www.loc.gov/pictures/

★ Index ★

Page numbers in *italics* indicate pictures

★ A

Adams, Abigail, 16, 21
Adams, John, 16, 17, 21, 28, 41
Adams, John Quincy, 38, 41, 53
African Americans, 77, 108–109, 113–114. *See also* antislavery movement
Air Force One, 101
airports, 100–102
Akin, Amanda, 69–70
Alexandria, Virginia, 2, 4, 22, 55
Alexandria Canal, 28
American Party. *See* Know-Nothing Party
Anacostia River bridge, 29
Anderson, Marian, 108–109, *109*
ant infestation, 47
antislavery movement, 49, 51–53, *51*
Aqueduct Bridge, 28
archaeology (activity), 4
Arey, Everett M., 71
Argus (sloop of war), 31
Arlington National Cemetery, 80–81, *81*
Armory Square Hospital, 69–70, *69*

Army of the Potomac, 76
Arthur, Chester A., 38, 84
artifacts, 4
artifacts (activities), 4, 55
Assaomeck, 2
Atzerodt, George, 75

★ B

Bacon, Henry, 95
Bailey, Gamaliel, 48, 52
Baltimore and Ohio Railroad Station, 87
Baltimore and Potomac Railroad Station, 87
Bank of the Metropolis, 38
Bank of Washington, 38
banks, 38
Bao Bao (panda), 119
Barry, Marion, Jr., 116
baseball teams, 102, *103*
Battle of Bladensburg, 30–31
Battle of Fort Stevens, 72
Beall, George, 4, 5
Beecher, Henry Ward, 72

Bellhaven, Virginia, 4
Beltway, 110, 112, *112*
Berryman, Clifford, 94
bicycles, 40–41
Bladensburg, Maryland, 30
Blaine, James, 84
Blair House, 40
Blodgett's Hotel, 25, *25*
Bonus Army, 103–105, *104*
Booth, John Wilkes, 74–75
Botanic Garden, 80, *80*
Bowen, Sayles, 78
Bradley, Abraham, 21
Breckinridge, John, 64
Brent, Robert, 23, 25
bricks, regulations for, 23
bridges, 28–29, 112
Brooks, Livingston, 70
Brown, John, 59
Buchanan, James, 61
buildings
    engineers and (activity), 123

height of, 92–93

number of, 36

See also churches; schools

Bullfinch, Thomas, 35

Bureau of Engraving and Printing, 37

Burke, Billie, 23

Burns, David, 13

Burns, Marcia, 13

business licenses, 93

Byrd, Richard, 81

★ **C**

Cairo Hotel, 92

Calhoun, John C., 40, 55

canals, 28, 42–43

Capital Beltway, 110, 112, *112*

Capitol Building

burning of, 31, *33*

cornerstone contents for, 57, 60

design and construction of, 17–19

dome of, 64, 65

1793 floor plan of, *19*

reconstruction of, 35, *35*

Capitol Hill, 2

Carey, Mathew, 89

Carroll, Daniel, 6, 8, 31

Carroll, John, 10

cartoons, political. *See* political
cartoons

Castle, the. *See* Smithsonian Institution

Center Market, 78–80, *79*

Chain Bridge, 28, *29*

cherry trees, 84–85, *85*, 87, 105–107

planting (activity), 86

Chesapeake and Ohio Canal, 28, 43

Chevy Chase, Maryland, 110

Chevy Chase Land Company, 110

Chinda, Iwa, 85

Christ Church (Navy Yard), 38

Christ Episcopal Church (Alexandria,
Virginia), 4

Christman, William, 81

Chung, Connie, 23

churches, 38–39, *39*

city layout game (activity), 9

Civil Rights Act (1964), 114

Civil War, 65–74

arrival of troops in District of Columbia
during, 66–68, *67, 68*

celebrations in Washington, DC, at end of,
74, 76–77

end of, 73–74

hospitals, 68–70, *69*

letter writing during, 70, 71

C.K., Louis, 23

Cleveland, Grover, 42

Cockburn, Alexander, 31–32

cofferdams, 28–29

Columbia (frigate), 31

Columbian College, 40

Columbian University, 40

concurrent resolutions, 24

Confederacy, 63, 67, 72

Connecticut Pie Bakery, 89

Constitution Hall, 108, 109

Continental Congress, 5–6, 56

cornerstones, 16, 19, 36, 56–57, 60, *106*, 108

counterfeiting, 37

Cranford's Paving Company, 48

★ **D**

Dallas, George, 39

Daughters of the American Revolution
(DAR), 108, 109

Davis, Benjamin O., 23

Decatur, Stephen, 39

Decatur House, 39

Dickens, Charles, 48

diplomats, 119–120

District of Columbia

and Alexandria, Virginia, 55

diamond shape of, 11, 12, 55

governance of, 22–23, 25

naming of, 7

See also Washington, DC

District of Columbia Self-Government and
Governmental Reorganization Act (1973), 116

Division of the Mississippi, 76

Drayton, Daniel, 49, 51, 52, 53

Dulles, John Foster, 101

Dulles International Airport, 101–102, *101*

Dunn, Charles A. R., 92

★ **E**

Early, Jubal, 72

earthquake, 122–123

Eisenhower, Dwight D., 101, 122
Ellicott, Andrew, 7, 7, 9, 11, 12
emancipation, 70, 72
Emancipation Proclamation, 72, 113
embassies, 119–120
Embassy Row, 119
engineering (activity), 123
English, Chester, 49, 52
Evers, Medgar, 81, 113

★ F

Fairchild, David, 84–85
Farrakhan, Louis, 114
Federal Census, 111
federal government
  costs of moving, to Washington, 20–21
  and jobs, 105
  land purchases by, 11, 13
  selection of site for, 5–6
Federal Regulation of Lobbying Act (1946),
  120
Fillmore, Millard, 90
firecrackers, 38
fires, protection against, 25
First Baptist Church, 38
flag design (activity), 92
Fleet, Henry, 2
Foggy Bottom, 42, 47–48
Ford's Theatre, 74, 75, 76
Fort Stevens, 72, 73
forts, 67
Franklin Delano Roosevelt Memorial, 121

Franklin Fire Company, 57
Freedman's Village, 80–81
Freedmen's Bureau, 77
French, Benjamin, 57
French, Daniel, 95
French Revolution, 48–49
Fulton, Robert, 35

★ G

gardening (activity), 86
Gardiner, David, 47
Garfield, James A., 84, 84
Garfield, Mary, 84
Gaston, William, 10
genealogy (activity), 111
George Washington University, 40
Georgetown, 4–5, 22, 47, 59, 78
Georgetown University, 9–10
Gilbert, Cass, 108
Gilmer, Thomas, 47
Goddess of Liberty, 64
Godey Lime Kilns, 48
Gordon, George, 4–5
Gore, Al, 23
government. See federal government
Government Safety-First Special Train,
  89
Grant, Ulysses S., 72, 74, 76, 94
Great Depression, 105
Greeley, Horace, 77
Greenleaf, James, 13
Guiteau, Charles, 84

★ H

Hadfield, George, 19
Hallett, William, 18
Hammett, Dashiell, 81
Harding, Warren, 97
Harpers Ferry, West Virginia, 59
Harris, Clara, 74
Harrison, William Henry, 42, 47
Hayes, Helen, 23
Haywood, William Henry, 55
Height of Buildings Act (1899),
  92–93
Henderson, Archibald, 61
highways, 110, 112, 112
Hill, Silas, 59
Hoban, James, 16–17, 16, 19, 25, 34,
  78
Hodgson, Joseph, 22
hogs, 38
home rule, 114–116
Home Rule Act (1974), 116
Hoover, Herbert, 105
Hoover, J. Edgar, 23
Hoover Field, 100
horse racing, 38
hospitals, 68–69
housing shortages, 21–22
Houston, Charles H., 23
Howard, Oliver Otis, 77
Howard University, 77
Hsing-Hsing (panda), 118, 119
Hurt, William, 23

★ I

"I Have a Dream" speech, 114
Ickes, Harold, 108–109
Ihrie, Peter, 43
inaugurations, 41–42, *42*, 65

★ J

Jackson, Andrew, 41–42, 53
Jefferson, Thomas, 7, 18, 23, 41
Jefferson Memorial, 60, 105–107, *106*
Jefferson Memorial Commission, 105
jobs, 105
John Laird & Son, 47
Johnson, Andrew, 75, 76
Johnson, Lyndon, 114, 115–116
Johnson, Thomas, 6
joint resolutions, 24

★ K

K Street bridge, 28
Kennedy, Edward, 81
Kennedy, John F., 81, 101, 113, 115
Kennedy, John F., Jr., 23
Kennedy, Robert F., 81
Kennedy, Robert F., Jr., 23
King, Martin Luther, Jr., 114
Know-Nothing Party, 58, 59, 61
Korean War Memorial, 121

★ L

Lafayette, Marquis de, 38
Lafayette Square, 39–40

Lang, William, 4
Latrobe, Benjamin, 19, 35, 120
laws, city, 23, 24, 25, 38
Layman, Christopher, 5
Layman, Rachael, 5
Lee, Robert E., 72, 73–74, 80
Legion Bridge, 112
L'Enfant, Pierre Charles, 6–9, 11
Lepcio, Ted, 102
letter writing (activity), 71
Lewis, John, 114
licenses, business, 93
Lin, Maya, 121
Lincoln, Abraham, 64, 65, 66, 72, 74–76
Lincoln, Robert, 97
Lincoln Memorial, 95, *95*, *96*, 97, 108–109
Lincoln Memorial Commission, 95
Lincoln Monument Association, 95
Ling-Ling (panda), 118, 119
Little Falls bridges, 28
Lloyd, Thomas, 78
Lobbying Disclosure Act (1995), 120
lobbyists, 120–121
Long Bridge, 28
lottery, canal, *43*
Louis, Joe, 81

★ M

Madison, Dolley, 30–31, 34, 46
Madison, James, 30, 33, 34
Magruder, William, 59
malaria, 47

Mall, the. *See* National Mall (the Mall)
Mao Zedong, 118
March on Washington for Jobs and Freedom, 113–114, *113*
marches, protest, 112–114
Marian Anderson Citizens Committee, 108
markets, 78–80
Marquis de Lafayette. *See* Lafayette, Marquis de
Marsh Market. *See* Center Market
Marshall, John, 41
Martin Luther King, Jr. Memorial, 121
McMillan Commission, 92
Mei Xiang (panda), 119
Mellon, Andrew, 91
Meloni, Christopher, 23
Memorial Continental Hall, *50*
memorials, 94, 121–122
    designing (activity), 77
    See also specific memorials
Metro (subway system), 112, 116–118
Metro Center Station, *117*, *118*
Million Man March, 114
Millionaire's Row, 119
Mills, Clark, 95
Mills, Robert, 90
Mineral, Virginia, earthquake in, 122–123
Monroe, James, 35, 40, 41
Montgomery County, Maryland, 94
monuments. *See* memorials
Moore, Thomas, 22
Morris, Robert, 13

mosquitoes, 47
Moton, Robert, 97
Moyaone, 2
museums, 34, 53–55, 76, 91

★ N

Nacochtank, 2
Namassingakent, 2
name rubbing (activity), 122
Nameroughquena, 2
National Airport (Ronald Reagan
  Washington National Airport), 100–102
National Archives Building, 80, 111
National Archives records, 111
National Capital Planning Act (1952), 116
National Cherry Blossom Festival, 87
National Era (newspaper), 48, *49*, 52
National Gallery of Art, 91
National Institution, 53
National Mall (the Mall)
  making of, 89–90, 92
  photograph of, *90*
  walking tour of, 91
National Museum of Natural History, 91
National Museum of the American Indian, 91
National Park Service, 5, 76
National Pie Bakery, 89
National Zoological Park (National Zoo), 87,
  118, 123
Native American Party. *See* Know-Nothing
  Party
Native Americans, 2

Navy Yard, 31, 32, 35
New Deal, 105
New York City, 6
9/11 attacks, 122
Nixon, Richard, 48, 118
Noor (Queen of Jordan), 23
Northup, Solomon, 49

★ O

Obama, Barack, 42
Octagon House, 34, *34*
Old Stone House, 5
Oldroyd, Osborn, 76
Onassis, Jacqueline, 81

★ P

pandas, 118–119, *118*
Parking Commission, 77
Patawomeke. *See* Potomac River
Patriotic Bank of Washington, 38
Patterson, Eleanor, 106
Pearl (ship), 49, 51–52
Peary, Robert, 81
Pennsylvania Avenue, 20, 38, 40, *50*, 77
Pennsylvania Railroad, 87
Pentagon, 109–110, 122
Petersen House, 75, 76
Philadelphia, Pennsylvania, 6, 107
Philanthropist (newspaper), 48
photography (activities), 4, 50, 55, 97, 123
Pierce, Franklin, 64
pies, 89

Plug Uglies, 61
Poinsett, Joel, 54
political cartoons, 94, *94*
Polk, James, 53, 55
Pope, Francis, 2
population statistics, 5, 22
Potomac River, 2, 6, 25, 28, 112
Poulton, Ferdinand, 9–10
Powell, Lewis, 75
President's House. *See* White House
Presidents Park. *See* Lafayette Square
Prince of Wales, *120*
Princeton (steamship), 46–47

★ R

Randel Plan, 9
Rathbone, Henry, 74, 75
Ream, Vinnie, 95
Renwick, James, 54
Reservations A and B, 104, 105
Residence Act (1790), 6
resolutions, 24
Rice, Luther, 40
Richmond Examiner, 66
riots, 49, 51–53, 61, 64, 66, 105
Robeson, Paul, 108
Rock Creek bridge, 28
Ronald Reagan Washington National
  Airport (National Airport), 100–102
Roosevelt, Eleanor, 108
Roosevelt, Franklin Delano, 100, 101, *106*,
  107

Roosevelt, Theodore, 94
Ross, Robert, 31–32
Rudolph-Garfield, Lucretia, *84*
Rush, Richard, 53

★ S

Saarinen, Eero, 101
Safety Train, 89
Saito, Sakiko, *86*
Sampras, Pete, 23
Sayre, Francis B., Jr., 89
Sayres, Edward, 49, 52, 53
schools, 39
Scidmore, Eliza Ruhamah, 84, 85
scrapbooks (activity), 40
seal, of Washington, DC, 23
Second Baptist Church, 38
Segway Personal Transporter, 122
Senate District Committee, 92
Senate Office Building, 93, 94
Senate Park Commission, 95
Senate subway, 93–94, *93*
7th New York Cavalry, 66–67, *68*
Seward, William Henry, 40, 75
Silliman, Fred, 70
simple resolutions, 24
Smith, John, 2
Smithson, James, 53
Smithsonian Institution, 53–55
  buildings of, *50*, 54
  collection creation (activity), 55
social life, 38

Somervell, Brehon, 109
Sousa, John Philip, 23
speech writing (activity), 114
springs, as water source, 25
St. John's Episcopal Church, 38, 39, *39*
St. Patrick's Church, 38
St. Peter's Church, 38
Stanton, Edwin, 75
Statesmen (baseball team), 102
Stockton, Robert, 46, 47
Stowe, Harriet Beecher, 48
stratigraphy, 4
streetcars, 110
Stuart, David, 6
suburban areas, 110–111
subway systems
  Metro, 112, 116–118, *117*, *118*
  Senate, 93–94, *93*
subway tunnels (activity), 119
Supreme Court Building, 60, 107–108, *107*
Supreme Court scrapbook (activity), 40
surveying (activity), 12

★ T

Taft, Helen Herron, 85
Taft, William Howard, 81, 97, 102, 107–108
Tai Shan (panda), 119
Tauxenant, 2
Tayloe, Benjamin, 21
then and now game (activity), 50
Thornton, William, 18, 32, 34
Tian Tian (panda), 119

Tiber Creek, 42
Tidal Basin, 106
Tingey, Thomas, 31
tolls, 28
Tomb of the Unknown Soldier, 81
Topham, Washington, 79
Tork, Peter, 23
Towers, John, 59
trains, 87–88, 89, 100
transportation, 87–88, 100–102, 110, 112,
  116–118, 122
Treaty of Ghent, 34
trees, 77, 84–85, 87, 105–107
Troop, Robert, 2
Truman, Harry S., 40, 102, 115
Twining, Thomas, 20
Tyler, John, 46–47

★ U

Uncle Tom's Cabin (Stowe), 48
Union Army, 67–68, *67*, *68*, 72–74, 76–77
Union Station, 87–88, *88*
United States Botanic Garden, 80, *80*
United States Telegraph, 38
Upshur, Abel, 47
urban planning (activity), 9
US Army Corps of Engineers, 95

★ V

Van Buren, Martin, 39, 42
velocipedes, 40–41
Vermont Avenue, *50*

Vienna Convention on Diplomatic Relations, 120

Vietnam Veterans Memorial, 121, *121*
  name rubbing (activity), 122
Vietnam Veterans Memorial Fund, 121
Virginia, 1606 map of, *3*
voting, 114–116
Voting Rights Amendment (1978), 116

★ **W**

walking tours (activity), 91, 97
Walter, Thomas U., 64
War Department, 22
War of 1812, 29–30
Washington, DC
  city seal of, 23
  Civil War in, 65–74
  construction in, 19–20
  contribution to Washington Memorial fund
    by, 57
  design and layout of, 6–9
  destruction of, 31–32, *32*
  early history of, 2, 5–6
  early residents of, 41
  earthquake felt in, 122–123
  flag of, 92
  governance of, 77–78, 114–116
  growth of, 22, 36, 38
  housing issues in, 21–22

land development in, 11
nicknames used for, 21
photographs of, *52, 86*
rebuilding of, 34–35
sources of water in, 25
See also specific landmarks
Washington, George
  burial of, 56
  and Christ Episcopal Church, 4
  design of capital city and, 7–8
  inaugurations of, 41
  land negotiations by, 11, 13
  and Pierre L'Enfant, 6
  White House and, 16
Washington, Martha, 56
Washington, Walter, 116
Washington Airport, 100
Washington Bridge Company, 28
Washington Canal Company, 42, 43
Washington City. *See* Washington, DC
Washington City Orphan Asylum, 57
Washington Gas and Light Company, 48
Washington-Hoover Airport, 100
Washington Metrorail system. *See* Metro
  (subway system)
Washington Monument
  cornerstone contents for, 57, 60
  design and construction of, 56–58

earthquake damage to, 123
sketches of, *57, 58*
Washington National Cathedral, 123
Washington National Monument Society, 56, 57, 58
Washington Nationals (baseball team), 102
Washington Senators (baseball team), 102, *103*
watermarks, 37
Watt, James, 121
Webster, Daniel, 60
Wederstrandt, Philemon Charles, 10–11
Wheatland, New York, 57
White House
  burning of, 31–32
  design and construction of, 16–17
  1807 sketch of, *17*
  reconstruction of, 34–35
Whitman, Walt, 70, *70*
Wilkins, William, 47
Wilson, Woodrow, 89
Winder, William, 30
Wolcott, Oliver, 17
Woodrow Wilson Bridge, 112
World Trade Center, 122
World War II Memorial, 121
writing activities, 71, 114

★ **Z**

zoo, 87